nonli

MANUAL

MANUAL

nonlinear editing

patrick morris

Focal Press

OXFORD AUCKLAND BOSTON JOHANNESBURG MELBOURNE NEW DELHI

Focal Press
An imprint of Butterworth-Heinemann
Linacre House, Jordan Hill, Oxford OX2 8DP
225 Wildwood Avenue, Woburn, MA 01801-2041
A division of Reed Educational and Professional Publishing Ltd

 A member of the Reed Elsevier plc group

First published 1999

British Library Cataloguing in Publication Data
Morris, Patrick
    Nonlinear editing – (Media manual)
    1. Video tapes – editing 2. Motion pictures – editing
    I. Title
    778.5'235

Library of Congress Cataloguing in Publication Data
A catalogue record for this book is available from the Library of Congress

ISBN 0 240 51564 1

Typeset by Avocet Typeset, Brill, Aylesbury, Bucks
Printed and bound in Great Britain by Biddles Ltd,
Guildford and Kings Lynn

Contents

Acknowledgements

Any publication like this cannot be written in isolation, and help and guidance has come from many quarters. I would like to extend special thanks to Chua Beng Teck of the Television Corporation of Singapore, Chris Wherry of Chris Wherry Audio and Ian Harrold of RealTime Productions.

Introduction

'Nonlinear' is a buzzword for every broadcaster and facility house worldwide. Systems range from the humble to the exotic, but all of these systems exhibit similar characteristics – they have areas where they excel and they also have common limitations.

This manual highlights those areas where nonlinear excels but at the same time introduces readers to its limitations. These limitations should be seen not so much as being a problem but as issues that need to be managed.

In many ways there has been a convergence of skills and technology, for nonlinear editing in itself is not new. Film was the original nonlinear post-production medium and all the skills the film editor has developed over nearly a century are now being learnt by the newer breed of videotape editors. At the same time, film editors are moving away from the conventional flat-bed systems and joining their tape-based colleagues and editing a comprehensive range of productions on computerized nonlinear systems. Computerized nonlinear systems have been used to edit feature films, documentaries, drama, light entertainment, news, current affairs, trailers, commercials and even programme censorship! All of which has been achieved on the ubiquitous desktop computer.

While primarily intended as a manual for professionals in the post-production industry, it will also serve as a guide to producers and directors and students of the broadcast industry. It is not intended as a 'techie' manual, although some technical aspects will be covered. The focus is also directed more at video rather than film for a number of reasons. First, a number of books exist that cover film comprehensively (see the recommended reading at the end of this book). Second, video is still the major medium of production within the television industry and nonlinear editing has completely changed the way of working.

Despite the growing acceptance of nonlinear editing systems many users, both new and experienced, complain about the complexity of operation, the time spent loading material into the system or the time spent rendering effects. This manual will hopefully introduce a mind-set that will encourage the efficient management of what appear as problem areas and at the same time encourage the reader to explore those areas where computerized nonlinear excels.

Chapter 1

What is linear editing?

Before considering nonlinear editing, it is necessary to define what linear editing is. Linear editing is usually used to describe video-tape editing. The term linear editing arrived after the advent of computerized nonlinear editing and, while the designation may well have originated from some sales pitch, it has stuck and is in many ways an appropriate term.

Linear videotape editing is the copy or dub editing process where shots are selected and copied from the source tape to the record or edit tape. The term linear highlights the straight-line principle of editing on tape, where typically an editor will start with shot one of a sequence and then add shot two, then shot three and so on until the programme is complete. What must be remembered is that tape-to-tape editing is a real-time process, which means that a 10-second shot will take 10 seconds to copy from the source tape to the record tape. In fact the actual process is longer than real time when one adds pre- and post-roll times.

This in itself is fine, but problems start to arise when changes are made. For example, suppose there is a 50 shot sequence and the decision is made to replace shot 20 with a new longer shot, but at the same time shots 21 to the end of the sequence are to remain the same length.

There are solutions, but the two most common do impose penalties. One approach is to take the whole programme down a generation and at the appropriate point add in the new material, then continue with the rest of the programme. In effect the original programme becomes a source tape, known as a sub-master. This process unfortunately takes time and results in loss of quality especially when using analogue tape – although with digital tape multi-generation losses are not so much of a problem. The second solution is to add in the new shot at the appropriate point on the original record tape and then re-edit all subsequent shots to complete the programme. This process preserves quality but imposes a major time penalty.

The limitations of tape

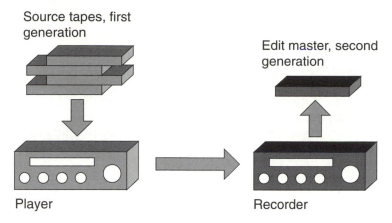

Source tapes, first generation

Edit master, second generation

Player

Recorder

Simple tape dub editing system with shots selected from the source tapes and copied to the edit master on the record machine

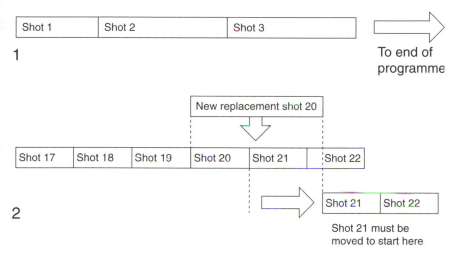

Shot 1	Shot 2	Shot 3

1

To end of programme

New replacement shot 20

Shot 17	Shot 18	Shot 19	Shot 20	Shot 21	Shot 22

Shot 21	Shot 22

2

Shot 21 must be moved to start here

(1) Shots edited in a straight-line process.
(2) Making changes to a videotape edit can be time consuming and impose quality penalties.

What's good?

- For just a few shots, tape-to-tape 'cuts' only editing can be very quick.

What's bad?

- As editing requirements go beyond cuts only, tape-to-tape editing can get expensive.
- If you change your mind then time and quality penalties will be imposed.

Using sub-masters

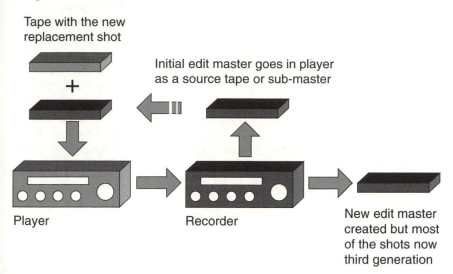

Tape with the new replacement shot

Initial edit master goes in player as a source tape or sub-master

Player

Recorder

New edit master created but most of the shots now third generation

Using sub-masters saves time, but in an analogue environment can lead to picture degredation.

What is nonlinear editing?

In some ways nonlinear editing is similar to linear editing. The common area is that source material (rushes) must be copied from tape to a new recording medium. The difference is that the new recording medium is a hard disk drive. During this process the off-tape video is converted to a digital format and recorded onto a hard disk drive. In effect the video is edited to the hard disk drive. The hard disk drives are usually external to the computer platform with sizes ranging from 2 GB to 23 GB. It is possible to daisy-chain a number of drives together to increase storage capacity. We shall see later that it is these hard drives that are one of the major limitations of nonlinear systems because you cannot have unlimited storage. This means nonlinear systems are not usually suitable for archive purposes. Wherever possible a programme will be loaded in, edited, downloaded for transmission and then the digitized programme material removed from the hard disk drives.

From here all similarities cease to exist. With all the rushes on the hard disk drives, an editor working on a nonlinear system enjoys the same increased flexibility that a typist does when changing from a typewriter to a computerized word processor. Just as one can copy and paste, duplicate, and move text around in a word processor, so one can manoeuvre sound and vision in a nonlinear editing system.

This cut and paste environment offers tremendous flexibility and speed. At the click of a button a shot can be replaced, lengthened or shortened at any time. Another advantage that these hard disk-based editing systems offer is access to multiple audio and video tracks and sophisticated editing tools. Editors transferring to this new technology may initially be apprehensive but invariably reach a point where they never want to see tape again.

When comparing linear and nonlinear, cost is also a factor. A typical linear videotape edit suite capable of performing simple effects, in addition to basic cuts, requires at least three videotape machines (i.e. two playback machines and a recorder). The installation also needs vision and sound mixing desks and an edit controller. The nonlinear system requires only one player/recorder and the editing system (usually a desktop computer). Overall the nonlinear system is cheaper to both purchase and run.

A basic nonlinear editing system

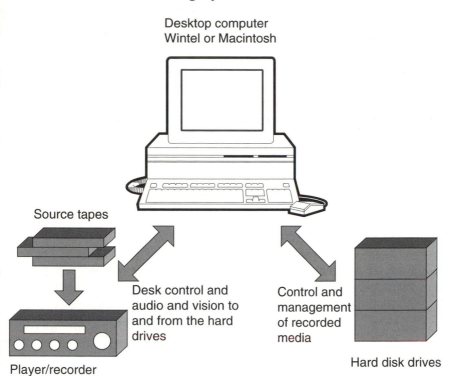

Desktop computer
Wintel or Macintosh

Source tapes

Desk control and
audio and vision to
and from the hard
drives

Control and
management
of recorded
media

Player/recorder

Hard disk drives

Usually the installation will include two computer monitors, audio monitoring
and sound mixing and a video monitor.

What's good?

- It is fast and flexible.
- It involves lower cost.

What's bad?

- There is a new and sometimes steep learning curve.
- Storage is a limitation and needs to be carefully managed.

A nonlinear editing system

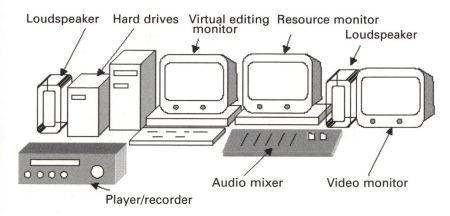

Loudspeaker Hard drives Virtual editing Resource monitor
monitor Loudspeaker

Player/recorder Audio mixer Video monitor

Professional systems offer two computer monitors – screen real estate is often at a premium. For quick access to all source material a dedicated monitor is recommended as a resource monitor. The video monitor provides real-time monitoring for quality control. In addition, video waveform monitors and vectorscopes will be installed

Chapter 2

Editing is primarily about telling a story, using pictures and sound to entertain, inform or educate. But if the quality, that is technical quality, is sub-standard the story may never get told. It could be that a broadcaster will not transmit a programme due to illegal colours being produced, or a client might object to distortion on audio. Whatever the reason, video editors need to have an understanding of the television system and the engineering criteria that apply to video and audio.

The interlaced scanning system

Video images are generated using an interlaced scanning system. An image is scanned from left to right and from top to bottom. Each complete scan from top to bottom is known as a field, which is designated as field 1 or field 2. The combining or interlace of two fields creates a frame. For the UK and most of Europe, the PAL system (Phase Alternating Line) has 312½ lines in each field and as a frame consists of two fields it is therefore made up of 625 scanning lines. The American NTSC system (National Television Standards Committee) uses 262½ lines per field and two fields per frame giving a total of 525 lines per frame. For the PAL system there are 25 frames per second and for NTSC there are 30 frames per second. In fact the NTSC system has a defined frame rate of 29.97 frames per second (see the discussion on timecode in Chapter 5 for more details). There is also the French system called SECAM (Séquential Couleur à Mémoire), which uses 625 scanning lines with a repetition rate of 25 frames per second.

The television scanning

A simple 11 line scanning system

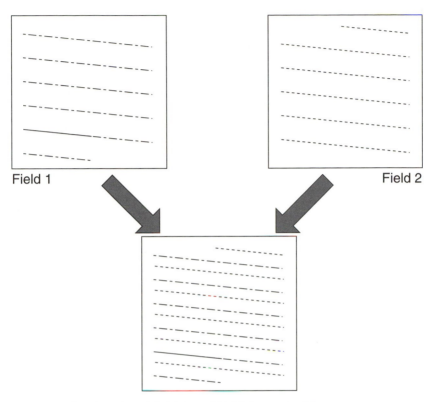

Field 1

Field 2

Composite of field 1 and field 2 equals 1 frame.
The two fields interlace when displayed

Two-field interlaced scanning. For PAL there are 312½ lines per field, 625 line per frame. The field repetition rate is 50 fields per second, and the frame rate is therefore 25 per second. For NTSC there are 262½ lines per field, 525 lines per frame. The field repetition rate is 60 fields per second and the frame rate is therefore 30 frames per second.

17

In the analogue world the signals generated are further defined to exist within certain parameters. Ignoring these parameters can lead to a loss of picture quality, which cannot be recovered.

The waveform monitor

A waveform monitor measures the brightness, or luminance, of the video signal. This device is used to confirm that illegal levels of luminance are not being generated, which is an important issue whether recording to tape or hard disks. The parameters of the PAL system define a 1 V signal with peak white at a maximum level of 0.7 V, colour black at 0 V and sync bottom at –0.3 V. While the scales and graticules vary from manufacturer to manufacturer, the essential criterion is that the maximum excursion of peak white should be no greater than 0.7 V from black level.

The vectorscope

The vectorscope is another electronic window into what is happening with the video signal. Its primary function is to measure levels of the colour, or chrominance, part of the signal. The most common signal to use as a reference is colour bars and there are a number of internationally agreed standards for a range of colour bar test signals. For PAL there are three: 100% bars, 95% bars and 75% bars. There should be one set of colour bars at the beginning of each tape, usually 75% or 100% bars. When viewed with a vectorscope the colour bars should conform to defined levels for hue and saturation, where hue is the colour and saturation is the depth of colour. For both PAL and NTSC there are prescribed safe colours and defined maxima for the saturation. A vectorscope is very important to check that the above parameters are not exceeded otherwise the reproduced colour in a domestic TV will not match that at the point of origination.

Colour bar waveforms

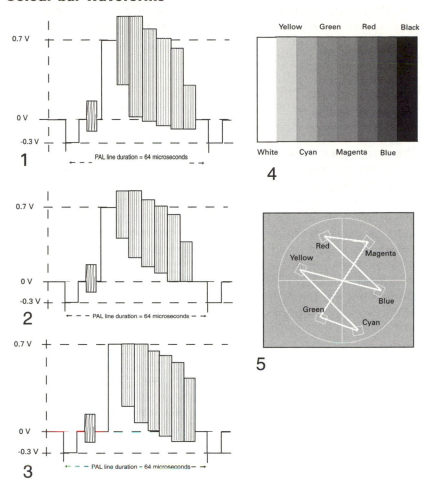

1 — PAL line duration = 64 microseconds

2 — PAL line duration = 64 microseconds

3 — PAL line duration = 64 microseconds

4 — Yellow | Green | Red | Black | White | Cyan | Magenta | Blue

5

(1) 100.0.100.0 colour bars more commonly known as 100% bars. (2) 100.0.100.25 colour bars more commonly known as 95% bars. (3) 100.0.75.0 colour bars more commonly known as 75% bars.

(4) Colour order as seen onscreen. *Note*: 100% and 75% bars are the two most common line-up signals found in post-production. Many colour bar types exist but they will normally offer a similar set of line-up reference points. (5) Colour bars as viewed on a vectorscope.

The video monitor

The TV monitor provides a representation of what the viewer will actually see. It is a quality indicator of both source material and completed programmes. The video monitors in any edit suite should be the best that can be afforded as, if the monitor is old or poorly lined up, it can give a misleading and inaccurate reproduction of the image. Some editors have been known to apply colour correction to overcome perceived problems on their monitors, and subsequently that programme has been aired with a colour fault!

The computer monitor

Computer monitors use a progressive scanning system with many more scanning lines than either PAL or NTSC. Computer monitors can have more than a thousand scanning lines with a repetition rate of up to 80 full scans from top to bottom per second, with no interlace used. Because of this, computer monitors have a much higher resolution than even an expensive high quality video monitor. The computer monitor, when used with graphics programmes, can also reproduce a different range of colours than allowed for in the TV system. As a consequence you cannot reliably quality monitor your video image on a computer monitor.

Audio

Just as with video, care must be taken when capturing audio to the hard disk drives. Most nonlinear installations use an audio mixing desk to assist with the setting of levels and for the easy selection of sound sources. While video will invariably be sourced from one replay deck, audio may come from ½ inch tape, audiocassette, audio CD or even a microphone. Manually patching all these, as required, into the back of a computer audio card is not recommended. Even those systems that provide a breakout box can give problems after only a short period of plugging in and removing cables.

To assist with the control and monitoring of levels most systems provide some means of audio metering. Broadly there are two types of meter in terms of their visual characteristics. These are the VU or Volume Unit meter and the PPM or Peak Programme Meter.

Monitor scanning systems

TV monitor

Line scanning at
312½ per
field for PAL and
line scanning at
262½ per
field for NTSC

1

Interlaced scanning on a TV monitor relies upon both
the persistence of the phosphors on the screen and the
persistence of the eye, so that flicker is not perceived

Computer monitor

Line scanning at
1070 lines with a
repetition of 75 Hz
or more

2

(1) The interlaced scanning of a TV monitor.
(2) The progressive scan of a computer monitor builds the image with consecutive
lines. The line rate and repetition rate are usually higher than for a TV monitor.

VU meters provide a visual reading of the average levels and do not show peaks. Due to the slow rise time of the pointer, high level transients of short duration will be missed. To avoid distortion a VU meter should not be allowed to go above 100% or 0 dB. The PPM in contrast has a fast rise time and a slow decay, which allows for transients to be monitored. The PPM is often considered as offering a more accurate visual representation of what audio levels are actually doing. As such they are much loved when understood, though many audio recording engineers are equally passionate about the VU meter. While many mechanical versions of both VU meters and PPMs exist it is probably most likely that an electronic version in the form of a bargraph meter is what will be used within the nonlinear system. This is a software emulation of the plasma or cheaper LED (light emitting diode) bargraph meter. It should also be noted that with digital systems the scales of the metering will be considerably different from that found on analogue systems. What is important is that audio needs to be checked on a regular basis and if necessary adjusted during the capturing process. If an audio mixer is in use then this level adjustment is much easier than using the tools provided within most digital nonlinear systems.

With many productions not enjoying the advantage of a sound recordist on location (the OMO or one-man operation) many videotapes arrive in the edit suite with no line-up tone whatsoever. This is due to the fact that, while broadcast cameras will offer video line-up in the form of colour bars, no audio line-up is available. The cameraman without an audio mixer will not provide the line-up tone. For the editor there is no alternative but to check and adjust levels on a continuous basis.

Summary

The basic principle for both audio and video is one of unity gain, so what goes in, comes out. Otherwise, it's 'garbage in, garbage out':

- Check all levels – both video and audio.
- Adjust if necessary on input to the system.
- Use the best quality measuring equipment.

Comparison of meter types

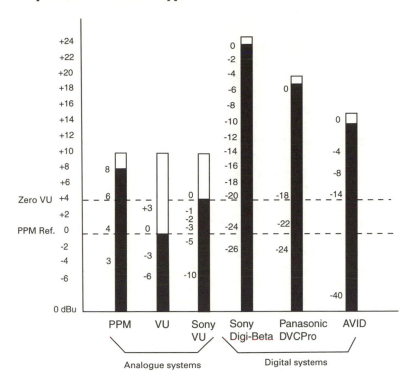

Guide for using VUs (avoiding distortion):
   The absolute maximum is 0 dB or 100% (remember short sounds may not be shown).
   Pure speech may have to be held back to -6 dB or lower (50% mod.).
   Some transient musical instruments hold to between -6 dB and -10 dB.
   Loud crowds or compressed material can reach 0 dB.

Guide for using PPMs (to help match the loudness):
   When using PPMs the audio levels may occasionally peak up to 6.
   Pure speech should be normally peaking 5 to 5$^1/_2$.
   Some acoustic instruments might be allowed to peak 5 – more complex music lower.
   Compressed music (rock bands, for example) need to be at a maximum of 4 and
     TV commercials may also need to be held at this level.
   Small crowds may peak 5, but very energetic ones only 4 or they will seem too loud.
   Background effects behind a voice should be held at approx. PPM 2 (or 3 at max.).

Audio metering has become very diverse. Check the manuals
for the system in use and establish a common practice.

Chapter 3

Digital signals and sampling

The apparent simplicity of a digital signal is centred on the signal having just two states, on or off, 1 or 0. This is unlike the analogue signal, which will contain many variations in levels which must be preserved in any processing. To generate a digital signal, samples of an analogue signal are taken as a series of numbers. This series of numbers contains all the information required to regenerate the original signal. Converting from analogue to digital is known as **coding** and reversing the process is known as **decoding**.

Sampling is performed at a frequency that must be more than twice the highest frequency of the signal to be sampled. For the ITU-R 601 coding standard this sampling frequency is chosen to be 13.5 MHz and accommodates differences between both PAL and NTSC. The sampling process will generate a digital number based on usually an 8 bit word. The size of the sampling word will determine the number of quantizing levels available. The 8 bit word or byte defined in the ITU-R 601 standard for broadcast television offers 256 levels, which can be used to describe a sampled signal. For our television picture, colour black is defined as level 16 and white as level 235. This leaves some headroom to accommodate signal variations that go either above or below the specified levels for black or white. This headroom is provided as digital coding, which can be very unforgiving in that signals that are too high in level will not get correctly coded into a digital equivalent. Hence the importance of proper attention to line-up when recording to either tape or hard disk drives.

Sampling

Byte size determines
number of steps, e.g.
8 bits per byte
offers 256 steps

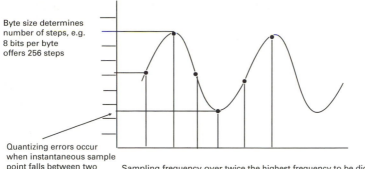

Quantizing errors occur
when instantaneous sample
point falls between two
quantizing levels. Usually
rounded down

Sampling frequency over twice the highest frequency to be digitized

For broadcast:
  video sampling frequency is 13.4 MHz
  audio sampling frequency is 44.1 kHz or 48 kHz

1

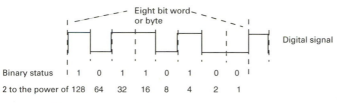

Eight bit word
or byte

Digital signal

Binary status	1	0	1	1	0	1	0	0
2 to the power of	128	64	32	16	8	4	2	1

Byte value =128+0+32+16+0+4+0+0 = 180

2

Maximum quantizing level

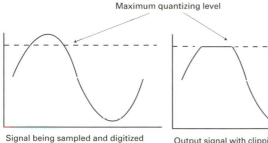

3   Signal being sampled and digitized

Output signal with clipping – all information
above the maximum quantizing level is lost

(1) The accuracy of digital processing is affected by both the sampling frequency and
the byte (word) size.
(2) Simple binary arithmetic.
(3) The pitfalls of allowing input levels to exceed the maximum quantizing level available.

Disk drives

There are two broad categories of disk drive. One is the internal hard drive of the platform being used – the C drive for Wintel machines and the system drive of the Macintosh. Here, Wintel has been used to identify the Windows/NT/Intel family of Personal Computers (PCs).

These internal drives are relatively small, from 1 to 4 GB, and contain the system software and details of the programmes being worked on. They are not usually used for storing the sound and vision (media files).

The other category of drives is those drives that store the media files or the digital versions of the sound and vision copied onto the system for editing. These drives are frequently external to the main computer, are relatively large and also need to be capable of high transfer rates. The transfer rate is the speed at which the drive can record and play back information to and from the computer. These drives for professional work invariably use a SCSI controller card, where SCSI (pronounced 'scuzzi') stands for Small Computer Systems Interface. SCSI comes in a number of varieties: SCSI 1 offers data transfer rates up to 5 MB per second; SCSI Fast offers data transfer rates up to 10 MB per second; SCSI Wide offers data transfer rates up to 20 MB per second; and SCSI Ultra Wide supports transfer rates up to 40 MB per second. The intended purpose of any system usually determines the type of drive supplied.

To increase the data throughput on drive systems, disk drives can be grouped together to increase the overall data rate. This process is known as **disk striping** or RAID (level 0) where RAID stands for Redundant Array of Independent Disks. So, for example, two Fast, Narrow SCSI disks (individual throughput of 10 MB per second) can be striped together to provide a throughput of 20 MB per second. It is usual to strip together matched pairs of drives, e.g. two 9 GB drives. While RAID pairing levels 1 to 4 offer data protection, RAID level 0 offers no data protection, so if one drive of a striped pair goes down all data is lost!

The external or media drives

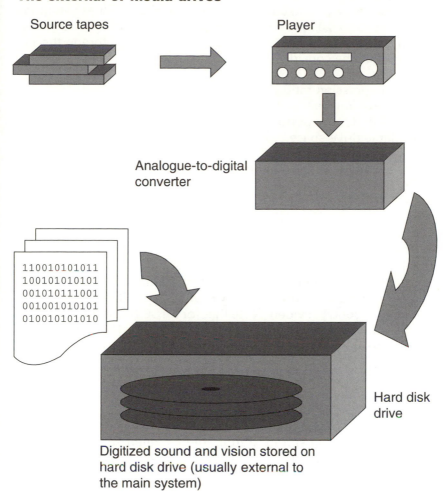

Source tapes

Player

Analogue-to-digital converter

110010101011
100101010101
001010111001
001001010101
010010101010

Hard disk drive

Digitized sound and vision stored on hard disk drive (usually external to the main system)

External hard drives hold the sound and vision in digitized form. Sizes range from 4 to 23 GB. Up to seven SCSI devices can be daisy-chained to a SCSI port. There are solutions to add more than the usual limit of seven devices.

Disk capacity

Hard disk capacity is usually given in units of GB. Values can range from 4 to over 20 GB. For an editor the concern is usually how much video a drive will hold. To assess available storage the following must be considered:

• the compression ratio or frame size in kB per second;
• the television standard (25 fps or 30 fps);
• the total number of tracks to be digitized (vision + audio);
• available drive space.

As an example the calculations for uncompressed video and audio are given.

Video

The total number of pixels per line is 720Y + 360Cr + 360Cb = 1440. With 576 active lines per frame this gives 1440 × 576 = 829 440 pixels per picture.

For PAL with a frame rate of 25 and a frame size of 830 kB, one second of video will occupy 21 MB of storage. One GB will store about 47 seconds of video. Note that for NTSC the storage requirements for each second come to the same figure. This is due to the higher frame rate compensating for the lower line rate.

Audio

Using a sampling frequency of 48 kHz and 16 bit sampling for audio, the storage is 48 kHz × 2 bytes (one byte = one 8 bit word) or 96 kB of storage required for each second of audio.

The difference in storage requirements when sampling at 44.1 kHz or 48 kHz is negligible and an approximate figure of 100 kB of storage for each second of audio is commonly used.

If compression is being used then the important figure to find is the frame rate for the video compression rate being used. Values from 15 kB per frame to 360 kB per frame are quite common. Most nonlinear systems will give an indication of how much capacity is available during digitizing, though the accuracy of these indicators is only approximate. One of the reasons is the use of variable frame size compression. Here the compression process will vary its frame size based on the complexity of the image being digitized with a complex shot having a larger frame size than a simple shot. Complex images are those with camera or lens movement or content that is very diverse. For example, a pan across a crowd

28

Approximate storage for video and two audio tracks

Frame size (kB per frame)	Single/two field	Storage per GB
15	single field	approx. 30 to 40 minutes
100	single field	approx. 10 to 25 minutes
150	two field	approx. 4 to 10 minutes
200	two field	approx. 3 to 6 minutes
300	two field	approx. 1 to 2 minutes

would be a complex shot to compress and digitize whereas a simple interview or talking head would require less processing to digitize and thus have a smaller frame size.

With off-line working, video frame rates can be reduced significantly by only digitizing one field of the video input signal, which is field 1. While this will reduce resolution it does offer increased video storage on the available drives. The image quality will be adequate for the editing process and as the output will be an EDL, the reduction in picture quality is a compromise with the frequent problem of available storage.

In any calculation on available storage, even when using the indicators available from the nonlinear editing software, the hard disk drive should not be completely filled to its maximum. As a rough guide, about 50 MB or 2 to 3 minutes of storage should be discounted. If this is not done there is the chance that access to the drive will be denied. The reason is that some headroom is required to allow database changes to be updated within the hard drive while an edit session is in progress.

Hard drives for audio and video require some headroom.
As a rough guide leave approx. 50 MB unused on a
9 GB drive

1

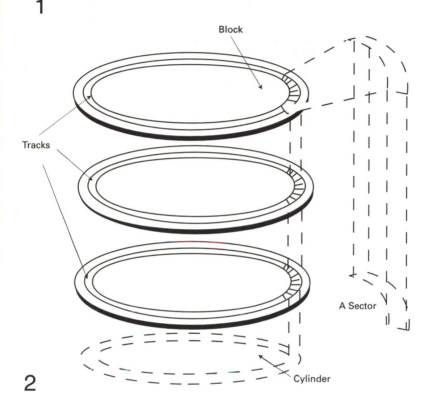

2

(1) With storage calculations allow some headroom for internal disk management.
(2) Parts of a disk drive. Data is stored as blocks on a track as part of a sector
and part of a cylinder.

Compression

Compression systems have evolved as a means of lowering transfer rates and increasing the effective capacity of hard disk drives. Video signals for broadcast are defined as wide bandwidth. In analogue terms the bandwidth is 5.5 MHz. Using conventional digitizing techniques every frame of broadcast video creates a file of about 1 MB – so one second of video requires 25 MB, which means that a hard disk drive needs a transfer rate of at least 25 MB per second. More importantly the transfer rate must be sustainable, which means that the hard disk drive must be able to maintain the specified transfer rate over long periods of time. It is important to read the small print carefully as some manufacturers quote burst rates, which only indicate a high transfer rate for short periods.

For broadcast video there are two broad categories of compression. One is the **intraframe** compression system and the second is the **interframe** compression system. Both attempt to address the issue of lowering transfer rates and increasing storage.

Intraframe

This compression system uses a mathematical algorithm that analyses every frame of video going through the digitizing process. JPEG is a common compression system of this type that is frequently used in broadcast professional nonlinear systems. JPEG stands for Joint Photographic Experts Group. This international body originally set about defining a compression system for still images. When JPEG is used for video it is referred to as Motion JPEG. As a compression system it is a lossy compression process, which means that picture degradation does take place. The level or amount of compression applied determines the overall picture quality. The level of compression is often specified as a ratio of the digital file size for the compressed video as compared with the file size with no compression applied. Typically the CCIR 601 component digital signal standard is used as the reference for uncompressed video. From this standard, uncompressed video is defined as 75 GB/hour for 625/50 PAL and 76 GB/hour for 525/60 NTSC.

Intraframe coding

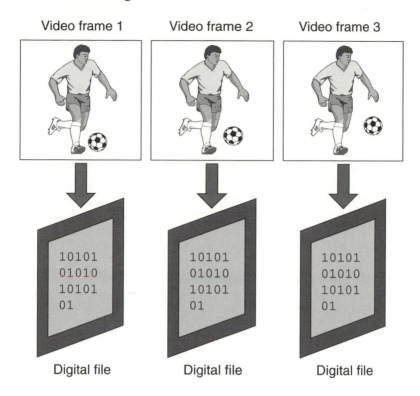

Video frame 1 Video frame 2 Video frame 3

10101
01010
10101
01

10101
01010
10101
01

10101
01010
10101
01

Digital file Digital file Digital file

Video frames converted to digital files on a frame by frame bases. Motion JPEG
intraframe compression.

Interframe

The Moving Picture Experts Group (MPEG) was set up in 1988 with the task of developing standards for the coding of moving pictures. This body has developed a number of standards. The principal ones, MPEG 1 and MPEG 2, both offer profiles that encompass the compression of video using an interframe process.

Interframe compression is an envelope type of compression, where a group of frames or group of pictures (GOP) are analysed and the subsequent digital file created is made up of both actual sampled frames and predicted frames. As a compression system it is very robust and frequently used for digital transmission systems. It also offers smaller file sizes for the same level of picture quality as JPEG and this feature has made it attractive for post-production. For the same picture quality, but using a higher level of compression, greater storage is obtainable on any given hard disk drive. Figures of up to three times more storage available using MPEG coding are sometimes quoted. Unfortunately, the processing involved in interframe coding masks the true content of every frame until that file (the GOP file) is decoded and subsequently recoded. One possible way round this is to code all frames as intraframe within the MPEG process, but this offers very little advantage in terms of improved storage capability – typically of the order of 1.3 times better.

While solutions are available they can be more costly and at the present time interframe compression is not the preferred compression system for broadcast nonlinear editing applications.

Within the family of MPEG there are many different profiles, the two most common being MPEG 1 and MPEG 2. Both compression systems are within the interframe category: MPEG 1 is the standard for video CDs (VHS picture quality) while MPEG 2 offers picture quality up to HDTV (High Definition Television). Of specific interest to post-production is the MPEG profile known as 422 Profile, Main Level or 422P@ML. The development of this profile is very likely to have a major impact on nonlinear editing systems. It offers solutions to all the criticisms of JPEG and earlier profiles of MPEG 2 plus, and most significantly, the possibility of some degree of standardization of digitized files. This would offer greater mobility of video files between applications and systems.

34

Interframe coding

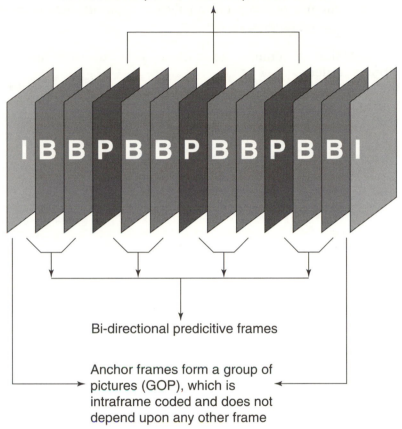

Predictive P frames – created from the difference between an input frame and a previous frame

I B B P B B P B B P B B I

Bi-directional predicitive frames

Anchor frames form a group of pictures (GOP), which is intraframe coded and does not depend upon any other frame

A group of frames are coded into a sequence where anchor frames are the only ones that can be decoded by themselves.

Summary

Digital technology promises the opportunity of generating a very robust signal for processing, manipulation and distribution. Limitations of bandwidth have imposed restrictions that have resulted in the use of compression systems. Unfortunately not all digital signals are created as equals:

- Compression is required to address both transfer rate and storage issues.
- Intraframe compression provides frame accuracy but is not the most efficient in terms of file size.
- Interframe compression is robust and used for distribution. Development is under way to resolve problems of editing in the MPEG 2 domain.

Problems of editing MPEG GOP

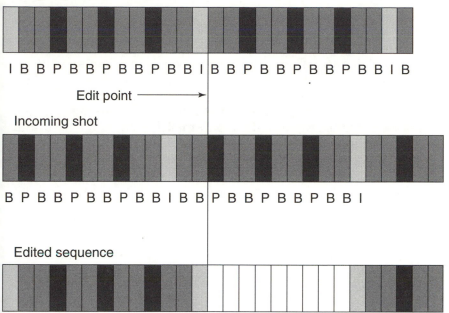

Outgoing shot

I B B P B B P B B P B B I B B P B B P B B P B B I B

Edit point ————————>

Incoming shot

B P B B P B B P B B I B B P B B P B B P B B I

Edited sequence

I B B P B B P B B P B B I ? ? ? ? ? ? ? ? ? ? I B B P

At the edit point the incoming shot has insufficient information available to recreate the first frame of the shot, as the incoming first frame is a predicted frame.

Chapter 4

Off-line and on-line editing

Off-line

Off-line editing is a process that has evolved from film and video-tape. In essence the editing medium is not the finished product but an intermediate process. For film this is a work print or a one-light print and for videotape low-end recording systems have been employed, for example VHS and U-matic. From both film and videotape the editing decisions are output as lists or text statements of what is required to make the finished programme. For film this is known as a **cut list** and for videotape it is an **edit decision list** or EDL. The actual programme will be created when the instructions in the cut list/EDL are applied to the original media.

With computerized nonlinear systems, working off-line usually means working at a low picture quality, using a high compression ratio (this is analogous to the one-light or work print in film and the U-matic/VHS used in video). By using a high compression, storage is maximized on the hard disk drives but still provides a vision quality that is good enough to make editing decisions. This is particularly useful when working on large projects like documentaries or a drama series. Working off-line offers the opportunity to have the complete series stored and available within the system. If a producer/director or even the editor needs to change the pace or feel of a programme it can be done quickly but with reference to all the relevant episodes.

The output is usually the edit decision list saved onto a floppy disk. This EDL can then be transferred to an on-line videotape edit suite where the programme can be auto-conformed by assembling the programme according to the instructions from the EDL. If it is a film project that is being cut off-line then the output will be a cut list.

The film and video process

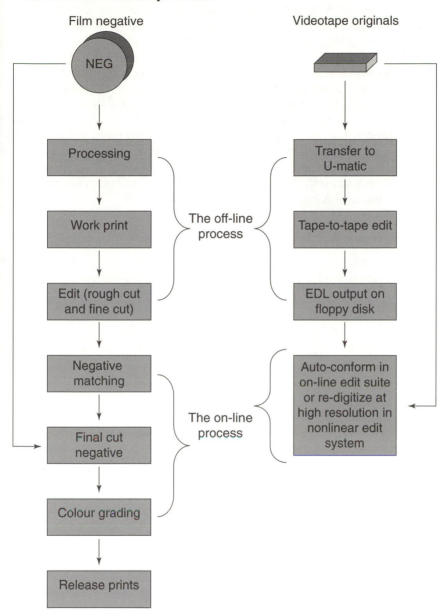

Note that in both sases the creative editing process is performed on an intermediate medium, the work print for film and U-matic or VHS for Video.

On-line

On-line editing is the process whereby the finished product is the on-air programme. Typically a compression ratio of 2:1 is used although in some environments, e.g. news, ratios of 5:1 may be used. Within the context of nonlinear editing many broadcasters are accepting the 2:1 compression ratio as broadcastable. There is a debate as to whether broadcastable is actually broadcast quality as most compression systems, including JPEG, are destructive so that even with mild compression of 2:1 there is some picture degradation. The acceptability of nonlinear systems to provide the finished programme is growing but the debate will continue as new distribution systems that use heavy compression in the transmission process will demand a very high level of technical quality prior to transmission.

The on-line process

Master source tapes

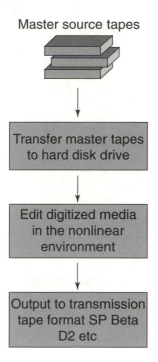

Transfer master tapes to hard disk drive

Edit digitized media in the nonlinear environment

Output to transmission tape format SP Beta D2 etc

Vision and audio transferred to disk at a high resolution. Edited and finished with visual effects and audio sweetening then output to tape for transmission. Some systems are designed to air direct from the hard drives.

The digitizing process

It is very straightforward to copy or digitize material into a nonlinear system. The system offers a user interface not dissimilar to a basic tape-to-tape editing system. The interface has controls for tape transport, a means for defining both what is to be recorded to disk in terms of audio or video, plus a means of defining how much or how little of the rushes is to be digitized. In effect the rushes are 'edited' to the hard disk drives. As some flexibility will be required during the real editing process it is usual to capture a little more of each shot than might be actually required. There are two reasons for this: to give some scope for trimming or adjusting the edit points within the programme; and, if effects are going to be used, even the humble dissolve, then some overlap is required from both incoming and outgoing shots.

This digitizing process differs from normal tape-to-tape editing in that the rushes captured are on a tape-by-tape basis rather than shots in any particular order. That process comes later. As well as the selecting tools, there are also tools to advise on the amount of storage that is available at particular resolutions depending on the type of project being worked on. If working off-line a low resolution or high compression ratio is used which maximizes the storage available.

When digitizing to the hard drives it is well worth performing a video and audio line-up, whatever compression ratio is being used. With a high compression ratio chosen the vision quality will be degraded to a VHS type of quality. If no line-up is performed one could reject shots due to apparent poor picture quality, whereas in fact the original was fine. If working on-line then a proper record line-up is a must, so the engineering aspect is important whatever resolution is in use. Ideally the system should have a vectorscope and waveform monitor attached so that picture quality can be monitored and adjusted to meet standard operating practices as appropriate, i.e. for PAL or NTSC. With more digital cameras being used the process of digitizing becomes a little more hands-off, mainly as input processing is not available on many nonlinear systems, so any adjustment will have to be performed on the playback deck or an external digital legalizer. These devices will alter the input signal so that no illegal levels are digitized. Audio is not usually compressed, primarily because it is not the enemy in terms of storage as it generates proportionally very small files on the hard drives. So a proper line-up procedure should be followed for any audio. As we shall see later, considerable savings can be made by treating audio as 'for broadcast' at all stages of the process (see Chapter 9 on Audio).

Digitizing

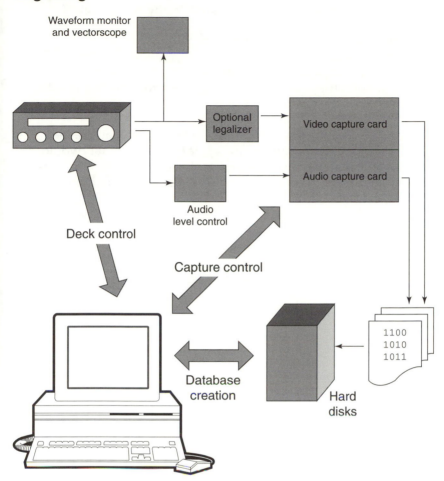

Waveform monitor and vectorscope

Optional legalizer

Video capture card

Audio capture card

Deck control

Audio level control

Capture control

1100
1010
1011

Database creation

Hard disks

When digitizing at high resolution with a view to finishing a programme for transmission, line-up of the audio and video is important. The technical quality of the finished item is governed very much by the input process.

As the digitizing process gets under way a database is automatically built. All systems create a record of the following:

- the number of tracks digitized (video and audio);
- the tape number;
- the marked timecode for the start of the shot (the 'in point') and the marked timecode for the end of the shot (the 'out point');
- the name of the shot.

While other fields may be offered or can be user created, the above represents a minimum of information that would be required to create an accurate and usable edit decision list. The following is a typical selection of additional fields that may be offered:

- the date and time of digitizing;
- which hard drive the file for each shot has been recorded to;
- the recording resolution chosen for each shot;
- the programme to which the shot belongs.

A simple database

Shot name	Tracks	Tape number	Timecode Start	Timecode End	Comments	Date

Logging accurately while digitizing or media logging can save considerable time. Establish a working practice that can be used with naming tapes and naming shots. In practice the database will contain extensive information, e.g. where the digital files are, duration of material captured and so on.

It is very important to develop good discipline in correctly naming tapes that are being digitized from and using workable and sensible names for the shots captured. User inputs are the tape name or number, and the name of the shot. If all tapes end up being named as 'Tape 1', the process of creating an EDL will be invalidated as during auto-conforming whatever system is in use will assume all shots are on just the one tape called 'Tape 1'! Timecode is a referencing mechanism for defining every frame on a tape, but a project may well have tapes with the same timecode. So the only way to differentiate between two shots with the same timecode is to qualify every shot with both the tape name and the timecode for that shot. In the event of two tapes having the same name/number, then just give one a new designation for the period of the post-production process. Do mark both the box and the tape. Chinagraph is a good way to temporarily mark a tape, so that confusion does not occur.

If you are ever unlucky enough to come across a rushes tape with the same timecode on it more than once (although a good cameraman will ensure that this never happens) your only safe solution is to re-timecode and then re-log the tape. If re-timecoding is not an option then take the tape down a generation and add new timecode.

If digitizing from some DV (domestic Digital Video) tapes then it is possible for the timecode to be duplicated on a tape. The tapecode on these systems (not true SMPTE timecode) will reset when changing batteries, changing tapes and de-powering. It is quite common for these tapes to be transferred to a professional tape format and then re-logged with consistent timecode.

Tape labelling

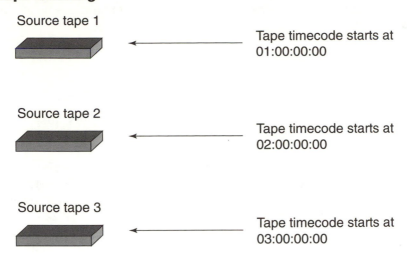

Source tape 1

Tape timecode starts at
01:00:00:00

Source tape 2

Tape timecode starts at
02:00:00:00

Source tape 3

Tape timecode starts at
03:00:00:00

If tapes 1 and 2 get digitized with the same name/number, problems will be encountered if an EDL is generated for on-line use. Number designations are usually best, as some on-line edit controllers will not accept letters as a tape name. If possible, arrange for the camera operator to change the hour of the timecode to match the tape – i.e. tape 1 starts 01:00:00:00, tape 2 starts 02:00:00:00, etc. If tapes have the same timecode then create a look-up list for the new designations you create for the tapes.

Some special cases
Some source material has no timecode, for example any of the following:

- audio CD;
- audio cassette;
- audio ¼ inch tape;
- VHS tape;
- DV tape (some do offer timecode, while others just offer tapecode, which can be zeroed at any point in recording!).

The best option is to transfer all such sources to a professional timecode format that your installation supports, e.g. SP Betacam, which allows the non-timecode rushes to be used later during auto-conforming. Even if the programme is being digitized as an on-line project, having all the rushes available on timecoded sources offers a little protection against either hard drive failure or operator error where digitized rushes get deleted by mistake! If they exist on timecoded sources, they can be reloaded as an automated process. While a little inconvenient, having the ability to automate all your actions from the digitizing and editing process can be well worthwhile.

Non-timecoded sources

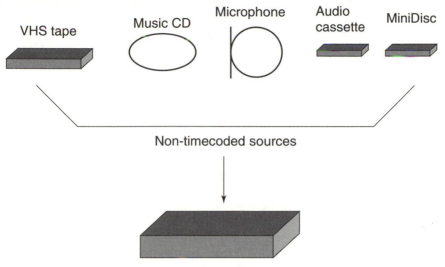

VHS tape   Music CD   Microphone   Audio cassette   MiniDisc

Non-timecoded sources

Compilation tape of non-timecoded sources

Some productions will require all non-timecoded sources to be compiled onto a professional timecode master. This could be for either the video on-line edit or for sound dubbing.

Editing

Given that nonlinear editing systems are designed to edit audio and video (or film), all systems offer controls/features that are a replication of their respective video or film environment. For example, there is a window or monitor for viewing the rushes, there is a window for viewing the compiled programme and there are controls for moving through the rushes or programme (transport controls). In addition there are the usual editing controls to define what shots to select and where to place them (mark in and mark out).

Nonlinear differs from a tape-to-tape environment in that many other features can be built within the 'virtual' environment. For example, multiple audio and video tracks can be created which can range from just two tracks to an unlimited number of tracks. But they are virtual and the maximum number of video tracks that can be replayed as a real-time process is usually only two. To replay multi-layered video tracks, a rendering process must be initiated to compile the multiple tracks into a single file for replay. For audio, depending on the systems configuration, 2, 4 or even 8 audio tracks can be replayed. With audio there is a further consideration that some systems allow up to 8 audio tracks to be monitored but only 2 audio tracks can be output to tape. Essentially this is a 'how deep is your pocket' problem, plus consideration of how the system is going to be used. A 2 input, 8 monitor, 2 output (2:8:2) configuration is not uncommon. With careful management by the editor this can be used effectively for many programme types.

In addition to the above, many other features can be provided including captioning, transition effects, and other tools to provide picture manipulation. For many editors, however, these additions are just a bonus – the real benefit of nonlinear is its speed and flexibility of editing material together.

To try to understand how this speed and flexibility is possible it is worthwhile understanding what the virtual environment of a nonlinear system is actually doing. First, the video and sound stored on the hard disk drives just sit there. During the editing process the system does not actually copy media from one part of a disk to another. When a shot is selected and edited into the record/edit monitor, all that happens is that a simple statement is created. This statement will indicate which shot (defined by timecode in and timecode out) was used, if it has sound with it and which tracks, and where it is in the programme being made. When it comes to playing this 'statement' the system looks up the appro-

The editing environment

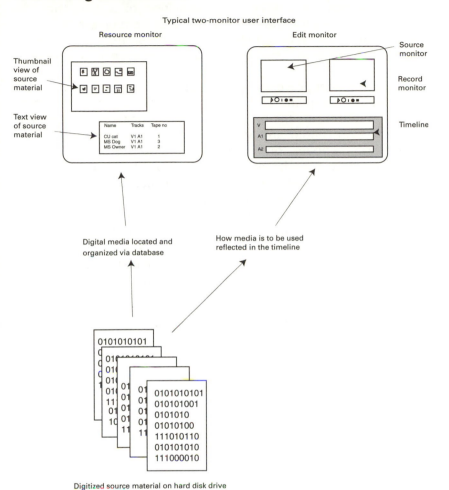

Typical two-monitor user interface

Resource monitor

Edit monitor

Source monitor

Thumbnail view of source material

Record monitor

Text view of source material

Name	Tracks	Tape no
CU cat	V1 A1	1
MS Dog	V1 A1	3
MS Owner	V1 A1	2

Timeline

V

A1

A2

Digital media located and organized via database

How media is to be used reflected in the timeline

0101010101
0101010101
010101001
0101010
01010100
111010110
010101010
111000010

Digitized source material on hard disk drive

The computerized nonlinear environment provides a virtual editing environment. Much of its power is derived from the database and the timeline.

priate shot at the correct point and replays it from its original position on the hard drive. At a transition to a new shot, the system then looks for and replays that shot from wherever it is on the hard drive. In essence the media just sit on the drives and are replayed as required. They are not recopied as each edit decision is made.

One of the most powerful features of all nonlinear systems is the **timeline**. The timeline is a graphic representation of the statement that represents the programme being made. It is possible to drag and drop audio and vision direct to the timeline and get immediate feedback on how the programme has changed. Remember that any selected shots just sit on the hard drive and do not need to be moved, so the editing process can be faster than real time. A shot 10 minutes long can be selected and edited to the timeline in the same amount of time as a 5-second shot. Just as important, a shot can be removed from the middle of a sequence and the created gap can be automatically closed up. These basic features are very much the reason why nonlinear is popular with both film and video editors. This speed and flexibility offers new opportunities of creativity.

Before going further, it is necessary to define some common editing terms and how they relate to the nonlinear environment:

- **Mark in (or in point)**
  A term used to define where the editor wants a shot to start from.

- **Mark out (or out point)**
  A term used to define where an editor wants a shot to end.

- **Three-point editing**
  A process that allows the in and out points to be set on either the source or the master edit and one other point to be defined. For example, the in and out point for a piece of dialogue can be defined on the source with only the in point of where that dialogue should go being marked on the master edit. The fourth point, the record out, is automatically calculated based on the duration of the source.

Editing terms 1

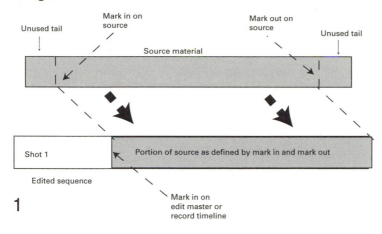

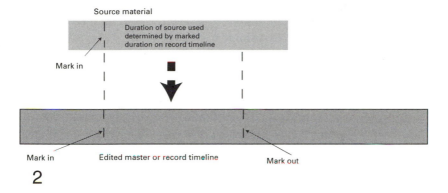

(1) Mark in and mark out points.
(2) Three-point editing can be referenced to either the source material or the record timeline. Typically priority will be given to the record timeline and if a marked in and out exists on the source the marked out point will be ignored (the exception being if four-point editing is enabled).

- **Four-point editing (fit to fill)**
  A process in which the in and out points are defined on the source and the master edit and a fit to fill operation is performed. For example, a shot on the source with a marked duration of 5 seconds when edited to a marked duration of 10 seconds on the master edit will apply a motion effect to match durations.

Usually the four-point edit is an option that needs to be enabled in some way depending on the software concerned.

More commonly if four points are defined the record master marked in and out points will take priority followed by the marked in or out of the source. So in the above example even if 5 seconds was defined on the source the record master will take 10 seconds as defined on the record master, ignoring the out point marked on the source.

- **Splice (insert)**
  A film type of operation whereby a shot edited into the programme as a splice will open the programme for the duration of the source material, thereby increasing the programme duration.

This type of edit offers great potential and is not possible on tape-based systems (although it could have been performed on the very first broadcast video recorders – the Quadraplex machine from Ampex).

- **Over-record (overlay, overwrite)**
  A process whereby source material is placed in the programme and removes or replaces what was originally there for the duration of the source material used. This process will not increase programme duration.

Editing terms 2

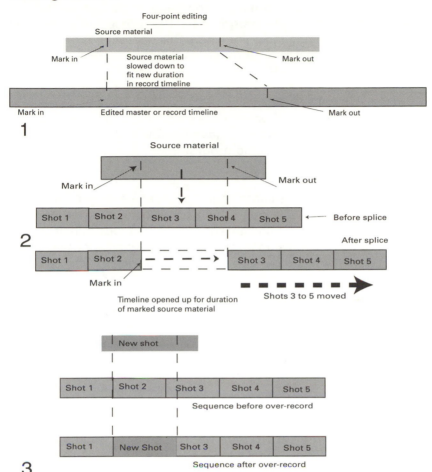

Four-point editing

Source material

Mark in   Source material   Mark out
            slowed down to
            fit new duration
            in record timeline

Mark in   Edited master or record timeline   Mark out

1

Source material

Mark in   Mark out

| Shot 1 | Shot 2 | Shot 3 | Shot 4 | Shot 5 | ← Before splice

2

After splice

| Shot 1 | Shot 2 | Shot 3 | Shot 4 | Shot 5 |

Mark in

Timeline opened up for duration   Shots 3 to 5 moved
of marked source material

New shot

| Shot 1 | Shot 2 | Shot 3 | Shot 4 | Shot 5 |
Sequence before over-record

| Shot 1 | New Shot | Shot 3 | Shot 4 | Shot 5 |

3   Sequence after over-record

(1) Four-point editing offers fit to fill. Usually not available for the audio.
(2) The insert or splice edit. Timeline opens to accommodate the new material.
(3) Over-record replaces any material that may have existed in the timeline.

- **Extract (remove)**
  A process whereby frames or complete shots can be defined and removed from the programme. This process will close up any shots following the point where this operation is performed. In general, programme duration will be shortened using this operation.

- **Lift**
  Removal of material from the programme and colour black and silence used to replace the removed material. This process does not alter the duration of the programme.

- **Transition**
  The change from one shot to another. It can be an instantaneous transition known as a **cut** or can occur over a period of time. This latter category is usually known as an **effect** transition and can be a two-dimensional transition, e.g. dissolve or wipe, or a three-dimensional transition, e.g. a page turn.

- **Trimming**
  A combination of most of the above can be applied to a transition. Frames can be added or subtracted from either side of a transition or from both sides. If both sides of a transition are being trimmed then what is added to one side in terms of numbers of frames will be removed from the other side.

- **Timeline**
  Part of the GUI, which will show the location of video and audio as it is edited into the programme. The timeline provides immediate feedback on what is happening as the programme develops and is a very powerful feature of all nonlinear editing environments.

Editing terms 3

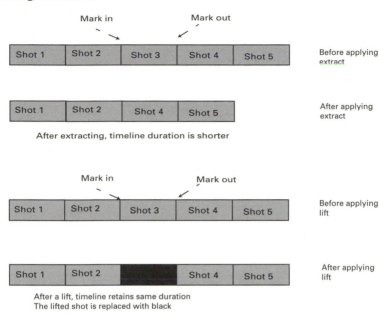

Mark in   Mark out

| Shot 1 | Shot 2 | Shot 3 | Shot 4 | Shot 5 |

Before applying
extract

| Shot 1 | Shot 2 | Shot 4 | Shot 5 |

After applying
extract

1   After extracting, timeline duration is shorter

Mark in   Mark out

| Shot 1 | Shot 2 | Shot 3 | Shot 4 | Shot 5 |

Before applying
lift

| Shot 1 | Shot 2 | | Shot 4 | Shot 5 |

After applying
lift

2   After a lift, timeline retains same duration
The lifted shot is replaced with black

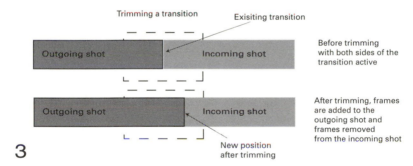

Trimming a transition   Exisiting transition

Outgoing shot   Incoming shot

Before trimming
with both sides of the
transition active

Outgoing shot   Incoming shot

After trimming, frames
are added to the
outgoing shot and
frames removed
from the incoming shot

New position
after trimming

3

(1) Extract allows single frames or any number of shots to be removed but the
timeline duration will get shorter based on the duration removed.
(2) Lift will allow single frames or any number of shots to be removed but leaves
the timeline duration untouched.
(3) Trimming is a combination of several individual tools all in one operation.

Output

The output options will largely depend on both the type of project and the resolution being used. The prime output options are:

- an edit decision list (EDL), plus VHS viewing copy of the programme;
- the programme at an on-line quality;
- digital files for use in another application.

EDLs

If working on an off-line project, the vision will be at VHS quality, and in fact it is not uncommon to make VHS copies as viewing tapes for producers/clients. But the real output at this stage is the EDL, which is a set of instructions that can be generated within the nonlinear system then saved to disk for use in an on-line tape edit suite. Care must be exercised in the generation of this EDL. One reason is that tape edit suites cannot understand an EDL with more than one vision track and more than four audio tracks (there are some exceptions – see Appendix B on EDLs). If there is a situation where more than one video track was used in the nonlinear system, then a separate EDL for each track must be made. Videotape edit controllers also work to different formats so it is important to make sure that the correct format is used when generating an EDL for use in a tape edit suite. The process of assembling a programme in a tape edit suite is frequently called **auto-conforming**.

On-line output

If the programme is a short form item, for example a trailer, then all digitizing may well be done at a high quality ready for output to tape direct from the hard drives. This disk to tape, or print to tape as it is sometimes called, requires the same output line-up that should have been exercised at the input stage. The principle is very simple: if you put X volts into the system then X volts should be output from the system without any variations. There is the proviso that no colour correction or adjustments have been made for creative effect.

Possible outputs

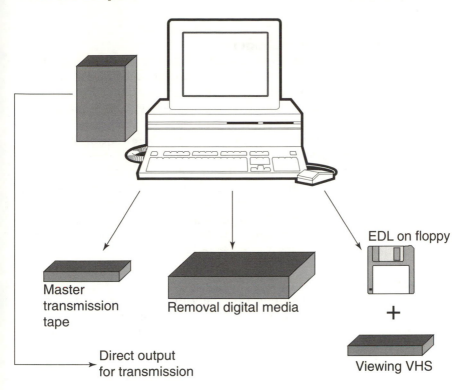

Master transmission tape

Removal digital media

EDL on floppy

+

Viewing VHS

Direct output for transmission

Output options vary according to the installation and the type of programming being undertaken. Direct to air can be found in news and on some stations for ident and commercial play-out.

Chapter 5

Project and system management

Editing in the nonlinear environment offers many new opportunities for editors to take control of the programme they are working on. A large part of this control is in how the project is managed. Nonlinear editing systems offer sophisticated data management systems, which will allow shots to be located by category (MS, CU, BCU, etc.) for rapid retrieval. It is in the management of the media that the editor has considerable control. As shots are captured and named a database is built up which, if created logically and with some structure, will allow very nearly instant access to all shots that are available on the hard drives and even quick access to those shots still on tape. To harness this potential fully, nonlinear systems make full use of timecode. Without timecode, video post-production would not be what it is today.

Timecode

Timecode is a digital signal, originally developed from telemetry systems to monitor space launches. Timecode quite simply provides a logging system that defines every frame on a tape by hours, minutes, seconds and frames.

Depending on the production, either time of day timecode will be used or a pre-set timecode for each tape. Time of day can be useful when covering sporting events as a production assistant can log the main action of the event by just looking at a watch without having to crowd the cameraman to monitor the timecode reader on the camera. Alternatively, a pre-set hour can be used to differentiate between multiple tapes within a production shoot, with the first tape of the shoot having a timecode that starts at 01:00:00:00, the second tape 02:00:00:00, and so on. This is fine until there are more than 24 tapes. Then each tape must have a unique name or number so that, at the auto-conform stage, the system will be able to tell the difference between two tapes with the same timecode. Two types of timecode exist: **longitudinal timecode** (LTC) and **vertical interval timecode** (VITC).

Media management

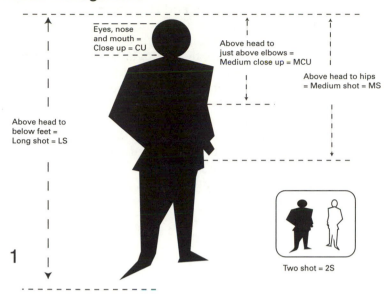

Eyes, nose
and mouth =
Close up = CU

Above head to
just above elbows =
Medium close up = MCU

Above head to hips
= Medium shot = MS

Above head to
below feet =
Long shot = LS

Two shot = 2S

1

Shot name	Scene	Comments	Tape	Timecode Start	Timecode End
WA John entering room	1	GT	6548	14:32:12:00	14:33:03:14
CU Janet reaction	1	GT	6548	14:45:21:11	14:46:10:01
CU Janet reaction	1	NG	6548	14:46:21:14	14:47:01:12
MS Janet John enters frame right	1	GT	6548	14:48:34:02	14:49:04:20

2   WA = Wide angle, GT = Good take, NG = No good

(1) Shot descriptions based on the human frame. Whatever system is used, be consistent.
(2) Sample text-based shot list.

LTC is recorded as a track on tape very much like audio. The code can be read accurately at play and shuttle speeds, but when in jog mode the information on the longitudinal track is not moving past the read head fast enough for accurate interpretation. In still mode, when there is no tape movement, the timecode cannot be read at all! VITC was invented to address this problem. Basically VITC is recorded as part of the video so even when there is no capstan movement, and hence no tape movement, there is video head drum movement against the tape which reads the video information and the VITC with it. Provided VITC is exactly the same as LTC, frame-accurate marking of shots can be maintained whether marking in or out points 'on the fly', that is at play speed, or in jog mode and selecting an edit point on a frame-by-frame basis.

Timecode

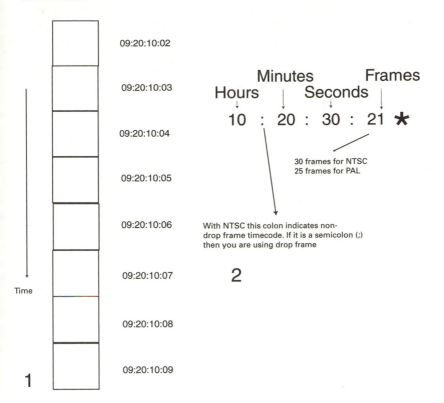

09:20:10:02

09:20:10:03

09:20:10:04

09:20:10:05

09:20:10:06

09:20:10:07

09:20:10:08

09:20:10:09

Time

1

Hours   Minutes   Seconds   Frames

10 : 20 : 30 : 21 ★

30 frames for NTSC
25 frames for PAL

With NTSC this colon indicates non-drop frame timecode. If it is a semicolon (;) then you are using drop frame

2

(1) Each video frame is time stamped with a numeric code based on the 24 hour clock.
(2) The timecode format – on some displays an asterisk will also be shown indicating field 2.

Drop frame and non-drop frame timecode

For NTSC there are two types of timecode: **drop frame** and **non-drop frame**. The reason for this is that the NTSC decided to define colour television signals as having a frame rate of 29.97 frames per second rather than the older standard of 30 frames per second, as used when timecode was first developed. Drop frame timecode is the newer development and makes allowance for the new slower frame rate defined by the NTSC. Within drop frame timecode, frame identifiers are omitted so that one hour of drop frame timecode will equal one hour real time. Note it is the identifiers that are dropped, not the actual frames. To achieve this the :00 and :01 frames are dropped at every new minute except for the 10 minute marks. So over an hour a total of 108 dropped references occur, which is a duration of 3.6 seconds, allowing the recorded timecode to keep track with real-time durations. The non-drop frame timecode works on a frame rate of 30 frames per second and therefore records longer durations than real time. So a tape with one hour of video using non-drop frame timecode will appear to have a duration of one hour and 3.6 seconds. Where accuracy of duration is of importance, drop frame timecode will be used – particularly on long form productions. Short form productions, e.g. commercials and trailers, which are usually less than a minute in duration, will be unaffected by the use of non-drop frame timecode.

Drop frame and non-drop frame

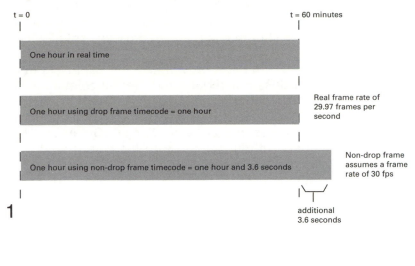

t = 0   t = 60 minutes

One hour in real time

One hour using drop frame timecode = one hour

Real frame rate of
29.97 frames per
second

One hour using non-drop frame timecode = one hour and 3.6 seconds

Non-drop frame
assumes a frame
rate of 30 fps

additional
3.6 seconds

1

Note the semicolon for drop frame and the missing ;00 and ;01 frames

| 02;03;59;28 | 02;03;59;29 | 02;04;00;02 | 02;04;00;03 | 02;04;00;04 |

| 02:03:58:28 | 02:03:59:29 | 02:04:00:00 | 02:04:00:01 | 02:04:00:02 |

Non-drop frame timecode maintains consecutive numbers across the new minute

2

(1) The real-time difference between non-drop frame and drop frame.
(2) The mechanics of drop frame timecode – the :00 and :01 flags are dropped on each new minute except at the 10, 20, 30, 40, 50 minute changeovers and at the top of each hour.

Operational problems with timecode

Problems can arise with regard to timecode. The most common is when a play/rec. has occurred in the camera without adequate pre-roll to the start of the shot that is required. Possible solutions are:

- Reduce the pre-roll if the system will allow it. Capturing into a nonlinear system does not require the normal colour framing procedure to be adhered to (particularly significant in PAL as it uses a 4 field colour sequence). The reason is that the nonlinear digital system captures and converts to Red, Green and Blue component signals without reference to the colour field information. It does not need this information, which is another plus as this means that any frame can be edited to any other frame. There is an exception, however. If the project is an off-line edit that will be auto-conformed in an analogue composite suite, then the EDL created should conform to the 4 field sequence of PAL.

- Copy all the problem tapes to new tapes with new timecode, and digitize from the new tapes.

- Digitize the material to disk but disable the deck control and timecode options. This is only recommended if working online. With no timecode, if anything goes wrong, it is very difficult to remount the programme.

- Try to make sure that proper discipline is applied on the shoot so that tapes do not come in with too short a pre-roll. While within the nonlinear system no pre-roll is required, the tape deck being used to digitize from will require a pre-roll, and if the programme is going to an on-line edit suite then having an adequate pre-roll will become a significant issue.

Operational problems

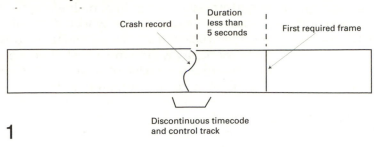

Crash record

Duration less than 5 seconds

First required frame

Discontinuous timecode and control track

1

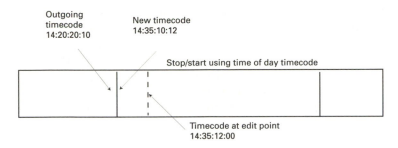

Outgoing timecode 14:20:20:10

New timecode 14:35:10:12

Stop/start using time of day timecode

Timecode at edit point 14:35:12:00

2

Tape deck will become confused as it pre-rolls past 14:35:10:12 to find 14:20:20:10, a jump of over 14 minutes. Frequently decks hunt and then give up!

(1) Crash record creates a break in control track and timecode, which prevents tape deck from replaying properly. First required action should be at least 5 or more seconds from start of record.

(2) Time of day timecode can create problems if a camera is stopped and started frequently. This can leave short duration shots that are difficult to cue up to due to the change in timecode.

Media logging

Media logging can be performed either at the nonlinear system or on a stand-alone workstation. Logging at a workstation has the advantage of removing the process from the edit suite as looking at rushes in the edit suite is not always the most cost-effective way to operate. Logging workstations consist of a playback deck, a computer, a video monitor and the logging software. Most suppliers of nonlinear systems either have their own software or can supply a third party product.

The logging process is just viewing and identifying what shots are on tape, then saving that information as a database in an appropriate format for import to the editing system. With so many people having gone the Wintel route in the office, but using Macintosh as the editing platform, there are software packages that will allow logging on a Wintel machine for import to a Mac.

If logging at a workstation, it is a good idea to log every shot as a record of what is on the tape. The information may not be needed immediately, but if the tape is archived that shot list will be very useful. When logging is complete the log can be saved or printed to hard copy as the tape shot list, then edited to create a digitize list. This helps to cut down on both digitizing time and storage requirements.

Media logging

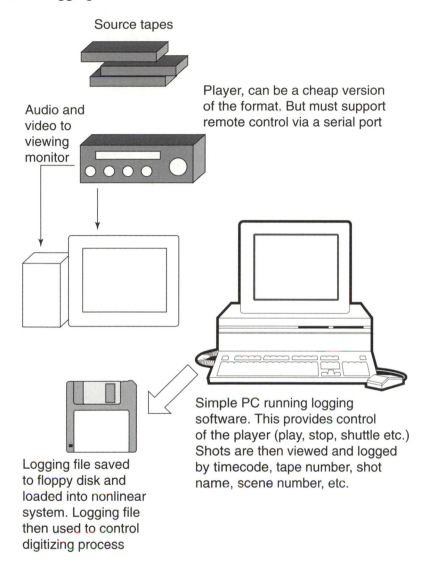

Source tapes

Audio and video to viewing monitor

Player, can be a cheap version of the format. But must support remote control via a serial port

Simple PC running logging software. This provides control of the player (play, stop, shuttle etc.) Shots are then viewed and logged by timecode, tape number, shot name, scene number, etc.

Logging file saved to floppy disk and loaded into nonlinear system. Logging file then used to control digitizing process

A simple and cost-effective method of shot listing all source material. A digitize list can be created from the shot list to automate the digitizing process.

Batch digitizing

Batch digitizing is the automated process of recording material to the hard drives. The system is controlled by a file that contains the following basic information:

- tape name/number;
- shot name;
- starting timecode;
- ending timecode;
- which tracks are to be recorded.

If additional information has been added, such as comments, shot number, take number, etc., this information will be carried over into the system but is not essential to the batch digitizing process.

Batch digitizing has two common uses. First, it is an efficient way of loading material on to the system, and second, it can be used to reload at a higher quality for finishing a programme started as an off-line project. In the second case the controlling file is the data built up in the off-line edit of what shots will be used and where. Typically all the low quality media used for the off-line are deleted from the hard drives and just the shots required to make the programme are then redigitized at the on-line quality.

Batch digitizing

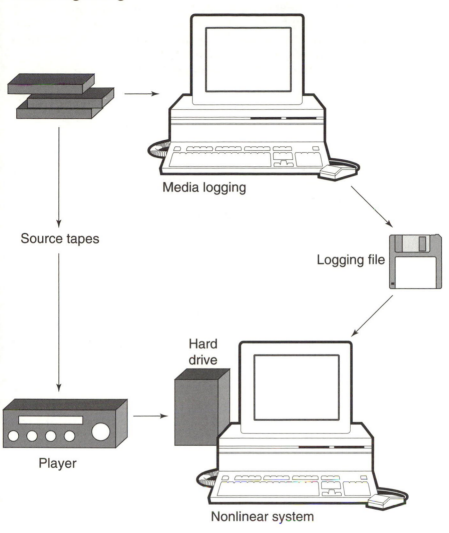

Media logging

Source tapes

Logging file

Hard drive

Player

Nonlinear system

Shot list or logging file created at a stand-alone workstation or on the nonlinear system, then used to control the capturing process. The system will ask for tapes by name then capture those as logged.

System management

Computer systems need managing and maintaining just as any other piece of equipment. Most problems will arise through software and operator error. Hardware tends to be less of a problem, although of course it can still fail.

The main items that need maintenance/protection are:

- the hardware;
- the software;
- the programme.

The hardware

Much of the hardware is not user serviceable, but there are some simple procedures that will minimize many of the problems frequently encountered. Make sure all cables are neatly laid out and securely connected. Many connectors have screw-in locators which should be screwed in properly (being careful not to over-tighten). Hard drive terminators should also be clipped in securely. Using a rechargeable battery supply can protect power. Such a battery supply will keep a system going even during a power failure, although not for long. Nevertheless, it will enable everything to be saved before shutting down. The perennial problem of coffee and tea is always with us – computers do not like drinks spilt over them, so take care!

The software

Both the system and application software can get corrupted. Be prepared to reinstall one or both if the system starts to get too erratic in behaviour. Of necessity it is a prudent idea to have the system and application software originals to hand. Complete systems have been known to be out of action for days while the engineering section searches for 'safely stored' disks!

Corruption of software can arise from internal bugs or from imported viruses. Internal bugs can only be reported to the software developers who will endeavour to establish a fix. Viruses are imported 'bugs' usually designed to corrupt the operating or system software. Installing a reputable anti-virus software can provide some protection, but only against known viruses. As new viruses are developed so one becomes vulnerable again.

System protection

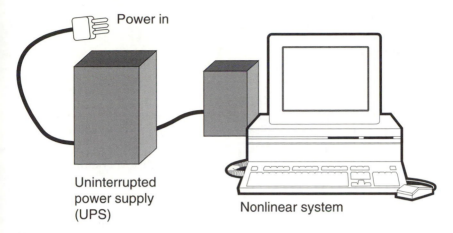

Power in

Uninterrupted
power supply
(UPS)

Nonlinear system

A UPS can provide protection against power failure. While the running time on a UPS will not be long, it is enough to allow a programmed shut down and saving of all work to date.

Virus infection can come via a number of routes:

- floppy disks and CDs;
- e-mail attachments;
- from the Internet.

The following strategies can help to minimize the risk of infection.

Identify the areas that interface with the outside world, as these are the most likely sources of viruses. Implement measures to ensure that files from the external sources are checked before they are brought into the systems.

Check unknown source disks on a 'sheep-dip' workstation. This is a stand-alone system where diskettes from unknown sources are checked. In the event of an attack, the damage is contained within this workstation.

Designate a set of diskettes strictly for use within the editing suite. Ensure that all staff use only officially designated diskettes. This can prevent people bringing infected disks into the system.

Run anti-virus software. This can run in the background during editing. If a known virus attacks, it will warn the user of an 'illegal operation' and offer the chance to save the project and then investigate the problem.

The programme

Taking the view that the programme is the most important item of all, back up in a regular and organized way. The most basic form of back-up is to copy the database information and the edited sequence database to a floppy disk. This is the information concerning what has been captured from which tapes and how it will be used in the programme. This should be done every time the system is shut down. For the short time it takes it could save hours! Note that it is the database information, not the actual sound and vision media, which is being backed up. This database information will be relatively small and can fit on a diskette. An auto-save facility exists on most systems, where the software will make a back-up copy of your editing decisions somewhere on the system drive while you are working, and can save a lot of time. It is well worth becoming familiar with where these auto-save files are kept and how to access them.

Possible routes for virus attack

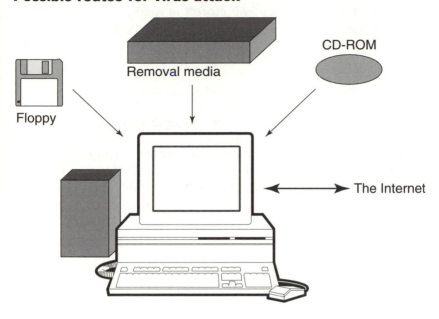

Any digital input to a computer system can potentially introduce a virus. Some protection can be offered by running some anti-virus software, but the best protection is to manage all inputs with care. Some viruses will corrupt media files!

On some systems it is possible to back up the sound and vision onto tape streamers which will store the media ready for reloading. This may be necessary if the editing needs to be spread over a number of weeks and other bookings need access to the system.

Summary

As with all things, preparation is all important:

- Establish a common and workable labelling system for tape numbering and shot descriptions.
- Media logging can save time as it automates capturing.
- Keep the original system and application software to hand.
- Back up frequently – it is a good habit that can pay dividends.

Programme protection

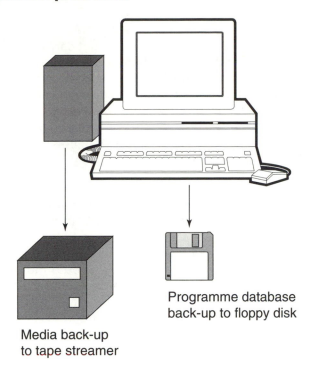

Media back-up
to tape streamer

Programme database
back-up to floppy disk

Computers can fail if programme information, i.e. editing and capturing database, is saved to floppy, then the programme can be remounted on another system. If the system supports tape streamers or similar archive medium, then the digital media files (sound and vision) can be backed up as well.

Chapter 6

When working with effects, it is very easy to get carried away and use effects just for the sake of using them. This is particularly true with the nonlinear system as effects can be applied as a simple drag and drop operation. There is not the space here to cover every effect that is available – rather, this chapter highlights a few problem areas that editors have experienced when first moving to nonlinear systems but have not had the benefit of working on sophisticated on-line tape systems.

Dissolve/wipe

The dissolve is probably the most used transition after the cut and is typically used to convey a movement in time and space. As an outgoing shot fades down, the incoming shot fades in. What is important and common to any effect used as a transition between two shots is the need to have some overlap of both the outgoing and the incoming shot. It is not uncommon for new editors to capture material very tight to what they require then cut the whole of the shots into the timeline. Where the user interface is of the AB roll type the need for overlap becomes more obvious, but on those timelines where effects are added directly to a cut, then it is less obvious.

If you are caught in a situation where all of the shot has been used, but the style is to have an effect on every shot change, then it will be necessary to digitize a longer version of the shots involved. It is possible to cheat by using your system to create media as a substitute for the lack of an overlap. The process is to create a freeze frame of the last frame of the outgoing shot or the first frame of the incoming shot. Edit this into the timeline to create the required overlap, so the dissolve will be from the freeze frame to the live action. Which frame you freeze will depend on the content of the outgoing or the incoming material. Try to create the freeze from that shot with the least movement within it for best results.

Basic effects

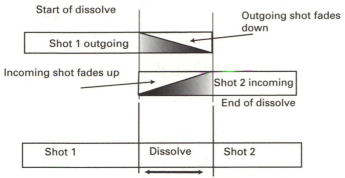

Start of dissolve

Shot 1 outgoing

Outgoing shot fades down

Incoming shot fades up

Shot 2 incoming

End of dissolve

Shot 1	Dissolve	Shot 2

Dissolve duration determined by amount of available overlap between the two selected shots

1

Outgoing shot	Incoming shot

Every available frame of outgoing shot on the hard drive

Every available frame of incoming shot on the hard drive

As every frame of each shot has been used no overlap is available for the effect to be applied

2

Outgoing shot

Incoming shot

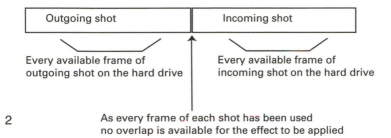

Last frame

Edited over the incoming shot to create the required overlap for an effect

Rendered to hard drive as freeze frame for say one second

3

(1) For even a basic effect like the dissolve an overlap of images is required.
(2) The problem of using all the material of a shot and not being able to apply effects.
(3) A possible solution by creating media within the nonlinear system, in this case a freeze frame.

Motion effects

At its simplest level motion effects are created by dropping frames (fast-motion) or repeating frames (slow-motion). In fact slightly more complicated algorithms are used to cope with a comprehensive range of speeds which can be adjusted in single steps of ±1%. The range offered is usually much greater than is possible using a videotape deck where the range is limited to +300% speed to −100% speed (where 100% = normal play speed). Your nonlinear system might well have a range as great as +9999 to −9999!

When choosing to create a slow-motion effect you will usually be given a choice of two or three options. One option is to create the slow-motion effect using 'both fields', another is to create slow-motion using duplicated field and a third is to create slow-motion using a sophisticated algorithm. The last option would be used when you have a complex shot in which there are both camera/lens movement and content movement.

When applying slow-motion to moving video the most common option is to use duplicated fields to create the motion effect. For example, to run an image at 50% normal speed, field 1 will be duplicated to create the effect. This does of course mean that the same information is being used twice in each frame throughout the effect so that with duplicated field the vertical resolution is halved. If both fields were used then a jerky motion effect would be created – quite fun for MTV-type programmes perhaps but probably not what is required for the normal slow-motion effect.

The two-field option is most effective when the image is static – for example, where a graphic has been captured to the hard drive from tape (say 5 seconds worth) but more of the graphic is required within the programme (for example, 10 seconds). To preserve the resolution of the graphic a freeze frame generated using both fields could be created and edited into the programme for the required duration.

Motion effects

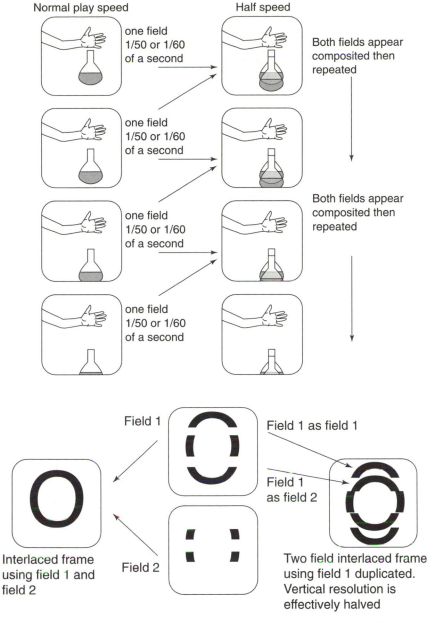

Normal play speed

one field
1/50 or 1/60
of a second

one field
1/50 or 1/60
of a second

one field
1/50 or 1/60
of a second

one field
1/50 or 1/60
of a second

Half speed

Both fields appear
composited then
repeated

Both fields appear
composited then
repeated

Field 1

Field 1 as field 1

Field 1
as field 2

Field 2

Interlaced frame
using field 1 and
field 2

Two field interlaced frame
using field 1 duplicated.
Vertical resolution is
effectively halved

(1) Video slow-motion using both fields will create a blurred and jerky effect.
(2) Using duplicated fields for motion effects reduces the resolution as the same
field information is used for both field 1 and field 2 on each frame.

Multi-layer effects

While most professional systems will offer real-time capability for effects, there are limitations, the most typical being that only two video streams can be replayed at any one time – for example, a full frame video background with a single picture-in-picture effect keyed on top. Although some of the more exotic systems offer greater capability, they will reach a point where the system is not able to replay all the information without intervention of some kind. That intervention is to render the effect into a single file. When the effect is required for playback, a single file, which is a composite of the effect, will be replayed.

While rendering does impose a time penalty, it should be seen as a procedure that needs to be managed rather than as a limitation. The simplest way to approach this is to consider seeing rendering as a separate function from the actual editing. It can be very tiresome to have to stop and wait a minute or so every time you apply an effect, so to overcome this, perform all the rendering at a time when you are not actually editing. Let the system batch-render all those effects while you are at lunch or having a coffee break. The rendering will take just as long, but while it is going on you can be doing something else.

Summary

- Simple effects are frequently available as real-time effects.
- Motion effects should be applied based on content. For slow-motion use duplicated field, for fast-motion use both fields, and for complex shots you may require a more sophisticated algorithm for smooth results.
- Design multi-layer effects in advance – if possible draw them out on a piece of paper.

Typical real-time capability

V2	Picture-in-picture effect – Aircraft taking off
V1	Background video – Man at train station

Composite output

Two video layers being replayed without rendering. To create more layers requires some rendering of the video material to a new file on the hard disks. With multiple effects, batch rendering can offer some degree of time management.

Chapter 7

Hole cutters

'Hole cutters' is a generic term which may be used to cover a number of techniques that are essentially image-compositing processes. The four techniques are:

- luminance key;
- chrominance key;
- matte key;
- alpha channels.

Luminance key

Luminance key is the process where a 'hole' can be cut in a background image based on the brightness of a second image. Historically, luminance keys were white on black captions, the white of the caption being used to cut a hole on the background video and then the white (or a colour from the vision mixer) being used to fill the hole. Luminance key is sometimes known as **self key**. In its simplest form a switching circuit would cut between the background and the key signal based on the luminance of the keying signal. Alternatively, any part of the image in the foreground that is at colour black will be transparent, the background image being visible wherever the foreground is black.

Many nonlinear systems will allow an image to be luminance inverted, or if necessary the image could be put through a graphics programme to perform an inversion that might be required.

Luminance key

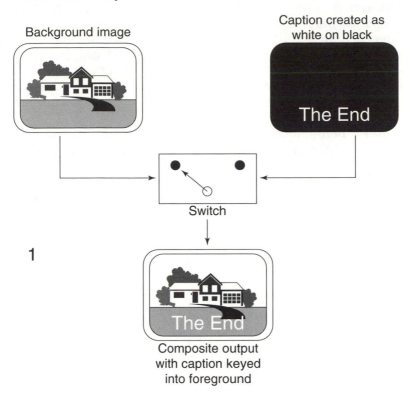

Background image

Caption created as
white on black

The End

Switch

1

Composite output
with caption keyed
into foreground

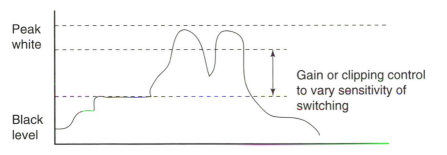

Peak
white

Gain or clipping control
to vary sensitivity of
switching

Black
level

2

(1) Two sources combined using luminance of foreground image.
(1) Keying controls will adjust for degree of keying so that detail in the black
does not appear in the foreground.

Chrominance key

Chrominance key is sometimes known as CSO (Colour Separation Overlay). This technique relies on colour to create the hole. Typically blue or green is used in television. As with luminance keys, two source video streams are needed: one the background, the second the chroma key foreground. A common instance where chroma key is used is with a television presenter. Here the presenter is shot against a chroma key blue background and keyed over either computer-generated graphics or a video image of a different location. The two, when keyed together, give a composite where the presenter appears to be in front of a background image.

While a presenter will usually be in a studio, it is not uncommon for magazine shows to shoot their presenters against a portable chroma key blue flip-out backdrop. This recorded video can then be chroma keyed over any background – graphics or video of a different location. In its simplest sense it is as if a fast-acting switch switches between the background and the foreground image based on the switching colour of the foreground image.

For any chroma key source, care must be exercised with the lighting of the background. If there are too many shadows from a presenter, difficulty may be experienced when trying to perform the chroma key in the nonlinear system. Depending on the sophistication of the system either colour suppression or colour ranging will be available. Colour ranging allows a range of colour to be selected to help with chroma keying – this is particularly useful when shadows exist on the chroma key background. Colour suppression offers a technique whereby blue colour fringing (typically on hair) can be selected and changed to a grey tone. The fringing is still there but is less objectionable.

As the digitizing process creates images based on blocks or pixels, the quality of any keyed effect will be dependent on the resolution used to capture all the necessary elements. For best results capture the video footage at the highest resolution possible to minimize any unwanted artefacts.

Chrominance key

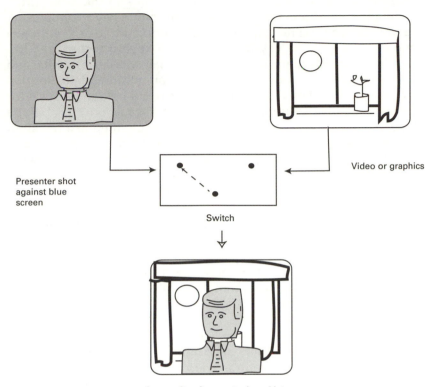

Presenter shot
against blue
screen

Video or graphics

Switch

Composite of presenter keyed into
foreground against video background

With good lighting and careful set-up excellent results can be obtained with chroma key. Not
all nonlinear systems offer real-time chroma key, while some offer the added sophistication
of colour suppression.

Matte key

Matte key is a two-element process: the fill and the hole cutter. Computer animations are one area where matte key may be used. If a production requires computer animation composited with live action video, chroma key and luminance keying techniques frequently are inadequate. This could be because blue, white and black all exist in the computer-generated animation. Matte key can also be applied when a scene to be shot could be dangerous – for example, a chase scene, where a car just misses 'our hero'. If the shot is such that the actor will be clearly visible then using a stunt man is not an option. So the scene will first be shot with the actor running through the shot, then the scene is shot again with just the car. In post-production a matte key is created that exactly maps an outline of the actor running – usually a white on black. This white on black matte key is then used to cut the hole on the shot with the car and the take with just the actor is then run synchronously with the matte key to provide the overall key.

Matte generation on desktop systems can be very time-consuming. The matte must match all movement exactly if the process is to be successful. This means that the white on black is created on a frame-by-frame basis.

Alpha channels

Alpha channels are usually associated with still images generated within a graphics programme, for example Photoshop. In some ways they are very similar to matte keys, in that an alpha channel will be a white on black (or black on white depending on the software) element within the graphic file format. On the Macintosh platform the most common file format used that supports alpha channels is the PICT file format. On a Wintel platform, the TIFF file format is a common choice. In both cases, to take advantage of alpha channels you must use the 32 bit option when saving a graphic from the graphics programme before importing for use into the editing system.

Matte key

First shot of talent

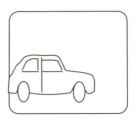

Second shot has just the car

Matte is electronically generated to work as the hole cutter

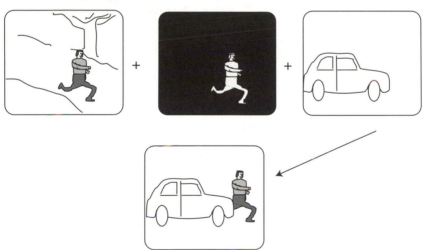

Final output compositing from three elements

Powerful technique for compositing moving images. While possible on desktop systems, the matte generation is generally created on a frame-by-frame basis and is time consuming.

Chapter 8

Working with titles and captions

Titles can be used to identify a speaker, a place, a time or some-times as translation. In fact, titles have many uses and there is not the space to cover all of them here. Rather, a guide is offered to the sensible use of titles and some of the pitfalls that can be encoun-tered.

For the purposes of this book, **titles** will be defined as text keyed over a moving background image. **Captions** will be defined as a composite of text over a colour background, a graphic or a still frame. This is by no means a universally accepted set of defi-nitions as, in many areas, titles and captions can be and are used interchangeably. A third category is **sub-titles**, which are usually used to provide a text translation or can be used for programmes for the hard of hearing.

The essential criterion for any title is that it can be read. That should be obvious, but there are a number of factors that need to be considered. Most importantly, to read a title takes time and the title must be legible.

On the matter of time, a good working guide for a name super is to allow a minimum on-screen duration of four seconds. If an address is being shown, for competition replies, for example, then read out the address twice to set a duration for its on-screen time – the information should be displayed on-screen for a sufficient length of time for the viewer to be able to write it down.

Legibility is frequently little more than common sense, but it helps if you know the language of the skill area you are working in. Like many specialized disciplines graphics has its own language and that language will be reflected in the software application used to generate graphics or text. Some of the most important terms are:

- point size;
- kerning;
- leading;
- font: serif, sans serif.

Titles and captions

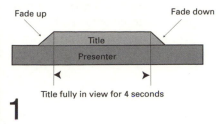

Fade up

Fade down

Title

Presenter

Title fully in view for 4 seconds

1

Joe Bloggs

Composite output

Start of full frame caption

Adjust outpoint to required duration

Read out loud the full address twice to determine on-screen duration

2

reply to:
Competition
Bloggs TV
Nowhere Town
BJ2 3PQ

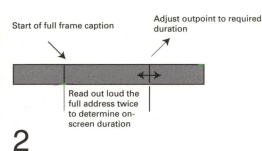

Captions should be kept to a format of five words per line with a maximum of five lines of text. (The 'five-by-five' guide)

3

(1) As a guide, name supers need a minimum of 4 seconds on-screen to be read reliably by a diverse audience.
(2) Address captions need a little extra time to allow viewers time to find pencil and paper and actually write down the address.
(3) The five-by-five guide is a reliable way of displaying text information on screen.

Point size

Text is usually defined by a point size, ranging from 6 point up to over 100 point. For print a common point size chosen is 12 point but for video, which is viewed at a greater distance than print, a point size of 12 will be too small to read. For video, point sizes of 24 and above are more acceptable.

Kerning

With some fonts the positioning of individual characters in a word will look unevenly spaced. Kerning allows for adjustment between individual characters. This can be done either on a word-by-word basis or on a character-by-character basis.

Leading

Leading allows for the adjustment of spaces between lines of text.

Font: serif, sans serif

One of the defining characteristics of fonts is based on whether the strokes that build up each text character have 'tails' or not. Those fonts offering tails are known as serifed fonts and those without are sans serif.

Remember that the screen you are using is a computer monitor and not a TV monitor. Also, it is probably a lot larger than that which many viewers will be using. With that in mind be cautious about using small point sizes and keep away from what might be called 'fussy' fonts. These are fonts that have elaborate but very thin 'twirls'. These thin aspects of a font, which might look fine on a computer screen, may be lost or poorly reproduced on the lower resolution of a TV monitor.

A good, solid and safe sans serif font is Helvetica. If serifed fonts are being used then use some form of text border or drop shadow, or a strap of some sort, to provide improved legibility. This is particularly important when using name supers. If an interviewee is wearing a white shirt and the name super is also in white, for example, without a border or drop shadow the text will be difficult to read.

Font characteristics

1 Text at 36 point

Text at 12 Point

TOWN — Before kerning
note apparent irregular
gaps between characters

TOWN — After kerning
gaps between characters
evened up

2

The space between
lines of text can be
adjusted by altering

the leading — Line spacing adjusted using
leading

3

This is Helvetica a sans serif font — A safe and popular font for video
which is sans serif

This is Bembo
some of the ornate strokes
could get lost when — While quite attractive some of
the detail of this serifed font
could get lost
reproduced on a video display

4

(1) Text size defined by point size.
(2) Kerning allows for adjustment of the space between characters.
(3) Leading alters the spaces between lines of text.
(4) Fonts – sans serif and with serif.

Style

Style is a very personal aspect of both text presentation and graphic design. In general, text is best presented in a consistent style. Keep to the same font, point size, use of shadow or a strap throughout the programme.

If text information keeps occurring in different styles the inconsistency could detract from the content of the text. Viewers may ask, 'Does a different colour of text signify something new?' So, if you are using pink colour fill for female interviewees and blue for male interviewees don't change your mind halfway through the programme!

With graphics imported from other applications, watch out for designs that have a lot of thin horizontal lines. These will 'buzz' on an interlaced television screen and need to be avoided. It may look good on the computer screen with its progressive scan, but the TV system may well display such graphics in an unsatisfactory manner. If possible a graphics workstation should have a TV monitor attached so that design criteria can be viewed prior to sending to a video edit suite.

Text style

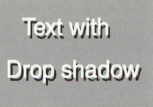

The addition of drop shadow can help with legibility. Quite useful when text is placed on a strap

1

Text with added border is useful in most instances

2

Text on a strap aids legibility considerably but may not be a good idea if it obscures too much of background.

3

(1) Drop shadow.
(2) Text with border.
(3) Text on a strap. Traditionally name supers and sub-titles are placed in the lower third of the screen. All text needs to be within the safe title area.

95

Working with third party graphics applications

The desktop computer at the core of many nonlinear editing systems provides the opportunity for additional software packages to be added or integrated to the post-production process. The most common type of additional software is graphics applications. There is not the space here to consider in depth this type of third party application but there are a number of general issues that need to be considered.

There are two main types of graphics: bitmap (or raster graphics) and vector graphics.

Bitmap

Bitmap graphics are quite commonly found in many graphics applications and are created by defining blocks (pixels) of information based on a grid. Bitmaps offer good colour range and subtleties of shading, but they do suffer from digital artefacts if resized. In particular, if a bitmap image is enlarged, a noticeable jaggedness will become observable.

Computer-generated pixels are square, though the digital standard for video (ITU-R 601) defines pixels as non-square. The number of bits allocated to each pixel defines the colour depth of each pixel. So a pixel defined by 4 bits can only have 16 colours. Computer graphics will usually offer up to 24 bits per pixel (or 32 if an alpha channel is supported). Unfortunately, the colour space on computers is based on RGB but the television industry has adopted the ITU-R 601 Y, Cr, Cb (luminance, red and blue colour difference signals). What this means is that colours created in a graphics package may not be accurately reproduced when imported to a nonlinear video editing system. In addition, allowances need to be made to accommodate the difference in aspect ratio of the two pixel systems (square and non-square). The PAL pixels are wider than they are tall and for NTSC the pixels are taller than they are wide.

As most computers create bitmap images using square pixels, the need to size graphic images prior to importing cannot be ignored. If no intervention is applied a circle generated in a square pixel environment will appear elliptical when imported to a non-square system.

On systems using an ITU-R 601 compliant capture card the frame size is 720 × 576 (PAL) and 720 × 486 (NTSC).

Bitmap images

Colour depth

Bits per pixel	Maximum number of colours
1	2
4	16
8	256
16	32,768
24	16,777,216
32	16,777,216 plus 8 bit alpha channel

1

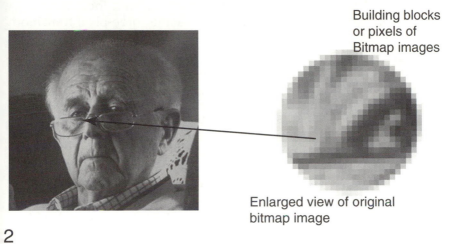

Building blocks
or pixels of
Bitmap images

Enlarged view of original
bitmap image

2

(1) Colour depth is determined by the number of bits per pixel.
(2) Building blocks or pixels of a bitmap image.

Vector graphics

Vector graphics (or object oriented images) are created by using mathematical formulae to generate curves and shapes. In essence, two or more points are joined mathematically, the shapes being produced having smooth curves with well-defined edges. Vector graphics are scalable without the problems of bitmap images, in that a resized vector graphic will not exhibit jagged edges and lines.

Any vector graphic going into a video application will have to be rasterized (or bitmap converted) prior to importing.

Anti-aliasing

The pixel building blocks of text will create a stepped pattern between the edge of the text and the background. To smooth out these aliasing edges, several mathematical processes have been developed to help reduce the stepped or jagged look of text. A common scheme of anti-aliasing is to add a three-pixel transition between the foreground and background as a means of softening the harshness of an edge.

Safe title area

Many domestic televisions do not reproduce the entire image that is transmitted. This is mainly due to something known as **overscan**. What is important is that allowance should be made for any text that needs to be reproduced and read. It is usual to find a mask available within a graphics package that will define what is known as **safe title area**. All text should be generated to fall within the defined safe title area mask. The safe title area mask will show a usable text screen area that is approximately 10% less than the full active frame size. In the case of a widescreen shot which will be delivered on a Digital Terrestrial Transmission system the network concerned may well insist on a smaller safe title area than one would expect for the widescreen production. This compromise safe title area is approximately the same as the normal 4:3 safe title area. If in doubt, check with the transmitting network. Unfortunately, the safe title area varies from network to network.

Vector graphics

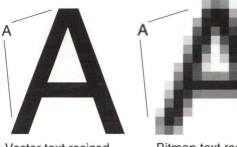  

Vector text resized
remains quite smooth

Bitmap text resized
displaying pixel
artefacts

Bitmap text resized
with anti-aliasing

1

2

Safe action area. Primarily
of concern to the camera
man and director to ensure
significant action is not
lost (5-7% of total)

Safe title area
Keep all text inside this
inner mask (7-10% of total)

3

NTSC frame size
720 x 486

PAL frame size
720 x 576

ITU-R 601
non-square
pixel frame sizes

(1) Vector graphics is a mathematical process offering resizing capabilities
without distortion. Vector graphics must be converted to bitmap for use in video.
Bitmapped images exhibit digital artefacts when resized. Anti-aliasing can
improve the look of resized bitmap images.
(2) Safe title area mask for standard 4:3 TV monitor.
(3) Digital frame size for 4:3 aspect ratio.

Saving time

One area where time can be saved is in the generation of basic text. Text such as name supers and end credit rollers can be typed up on an office computer and then saved as a .txt file. Any spell-checking can be done at this stage. This file can then be imported, copied and pasted into the graphics programme of the nonlinear system for formatting and editing into the programme. Using the nonlinear suite as an electronic typewriter is not particularly cost effective as it stops the editing process.

File type and cross-platform compatibility

Several file formats exist that offer cross-platform compatibility. Examples are GIF (Graphics Interchange Format), TIF (Tagged Image Format) and JPG (Joint Photographic Experts Group).

However, it is always prudent to stay within a common platform, as it is possible for some degree of degradation to occur when importing graphics from a different computer platform. This is particularly so when trying to convert a vector-based file format to a bitmap image to run on a different platform.

Summary

Graphics are becoming such a common part of the toolkit that editors need to be familiar with both their creation and their use:

- While beauty is in the eye of the beholder, in most cases keep the design simple and bold. Remember that any text must be legible.
- Having one box that does everything is not necessarily the panacea one might assume. While it may appear cost effective to have editing and graphics generation all on one system, remember that these systems are not truly multitasking. So if the editor is designing or creating graphics he or she is not editing.
- If a separate graphics workstation is used then try to keep to native file types. While cross-platform compatibility does exist, there is always the possibility of some image degradation.

Cross-platform compatability

File extension	File type	Colours	Platforms supported
BMP	Bitmap	Mono through to 24 bit	Windows, Windows NT
GIF89a	Bitmap	Converts RGB to 8 bit index linked colours	Windows, Windows NT, Macintosh
TGA (TARGA)	Bitmap	8 bits, 16 bits, 24 bits, 32 bits	Windows, Windows NT, Macintosh
TIF (TIFF)	Bitmap	1 bit, 4 bits, 8 bits, 24 bits	Windows, Windows NT, Macintosh
JPG (JPEG)	Bitmap	24 bits	Windows, Windows NT Macintosh
PIC (PICT)	Bitmap	4 bits, 8 bits, 24 bits	Windows, Windows NT, Macintosh

The above list is by no means exhaustive but does indicate a number of files
that have cross-platform capability. The GIF89a with only 256 colours (max.) does
support alpha channels. The Macintosh PICT file format also supports alpha channels.
Wherever possible it is recommended to stay in the same platform for image creation and
subsequent import into a digital nonlinear system.

Chapter 9

Working with audio

Audio has never enjoyed the 'glamour' of video, and consequently all too often it is not given the respect it deserves. In fact audio is just as important as video – and it might be argued that it is even more important.

A programme with some of the best pictures in the world can be unwatchable if the sound is distorted or muddled. Yet good quality sound with some suspect images can be watchable. Throughout the world this is an everyday occurrence with news. Nonlinear editing systems offer the editor all that could be expected from a tape edit suite and more, but if the audio has not been given the due care and attention at the acquisition stage then even the most sophisticated of systems or the most skilled of audio engineers can do little after the event. All too often for the sake of a few minutes on location, huge penalties can be imposed in the edit suite.

Nonlinear editing systems offer one major advantage over their tape-to-tape video counterparts. That is the ability to handle many audio tracks. While they exist in a virtual environment they are very usable. With television now stereo it is very easy to get to six or more audio tracks very quickly, but on tape you will be lucky to have four audio tracks available. This ability alone makes non-linear very attractive. Equally, if working with just a voiceover and effects, it is very easy to add audio cross-fades to the effects track to smooth transitions between different audio sounds. On tape this can be very difficult – though not impossible – but all too often an editor will just try to match levels rather than go through the required process of laying off audio to another machine to perform an audio cross-fade. The nonlinear environment offers the opportunity to add a little extra polish to audio with great ease.

Tape versus nonlinear audio

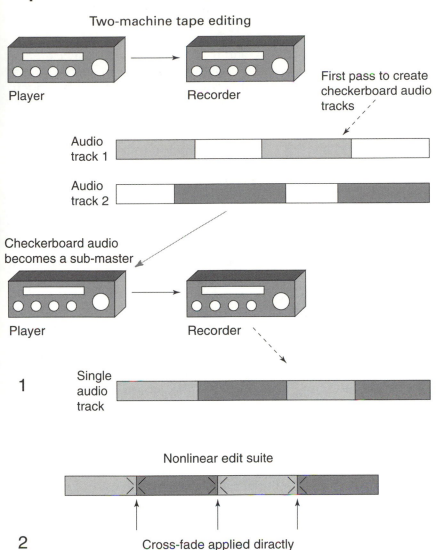

Two-machine tape editing

Player   Recorder

First pass to create checkerboard audio tracks

Audio track 1

Audio track 2

Checkerboard audio becomes a sub-master

Player   Recorder

1   Single audio track

Nonlinear edit suite

2   Cross-fade applied diractly in timeline and rendered

(1) Track-laying on a simple tape-to-tape edit. Requires two passes to complete the mix, or alternatively a third machine is required. Quite often editors will just match levels.

(2) In the nonlinear environment the cross-fade is applied directly and then rendered. This can also be performed globally by applying a cross-fade on any number of cut-together audio sources.

Audio options for the nonlinear suite

Audio captured to a hard drive during a nonlinear off-line session will be sampled at either 44.1 kHz or 48 kHz (make sure that all audio is captured with a consistent setting for the sampling frequency). In both cases the audio is being sampled at a broadcastable standard. This audio should be set up and monitored as if it was for transmission. If this is done, the audio can be edited and prepared for transmission wholly in the nonlinear system, although this will depend upon the type of programme and existing operational practices.

When an off-line edit is complete, the programme audio can be treated in a number of different ways:

- audio finish in the nonlinear system;
- audio finish in a sound dubbing suite.

Audio finish in the nonlinear system

Finishing audio in the nonlinear suite is quite feasible, provided care has been exercised during the capture process. There are many 'plug-in' software modules offering a comprehensive toolkit that can match a sophisticated purpose-built dubbing suite. These include, for example, advanced editing tools and audio effects. There are two points that need to be considered. First, all these specialized plug-in audio tools need to be understood and used with skill, as such an experienced dubbing engineer would be able to perform the audio sweetening much quicker. Many TV programmes require fairly basic sound sweetening such as adding music and some audio balancing, both of which can be done efficiently within a nonlinear system. The second point is that even simple sound balancing does take time and if the programme throughput is high enough then that time spent audio balancing might be better spent editing the next programme.

If the programme is going to be off-lined then on-lined within the nonlinear system, time savings can be made by finishing the audio at the off-line stage and only recapturing the vision at a high resolution to complete the programme. This will save a lot of time with audio line-up and trying to match audio sources to their correct location in the programme when they have not come from timecoded sources.

Audio finish on a nonlinear suite

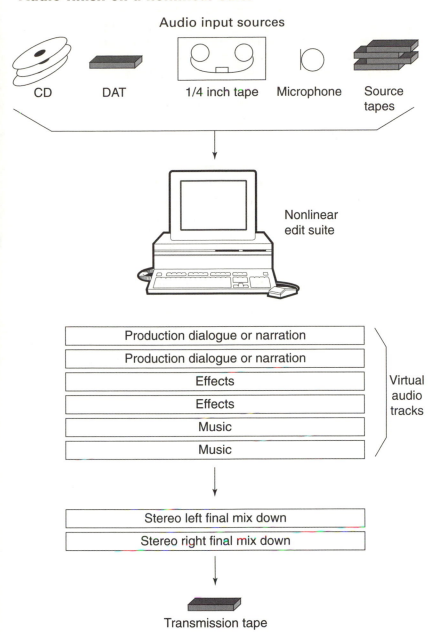

Audio input sources

CD   DAT   1/4 inch tape   Microphone   Source tapes

Nonlinear edit suite

| Production dialogue or narration |
| Production dialogue or narration |
| Effects |
| Effects |
| Music |
| Music |

Virtual audio tracks

| Stereo left final mix down |
| Stereo right final mix down |

Transmission tape

Audio inputs digitized and edited with sound sweetening using virtual audio tracks. The final audio is rendered or mixed down to a stereo pair for output to tape.

If the vision is going to be auto-conformed in a tape suite then the finished audio can be output to tape with the low resolution vision and the EDL generated as a vision-only edit decision list. The on-line tape suite will then edit the vision onto the finished audio as output from the off-line suite, which will typically save up to 30 to 40 per cent of the on-line tape suite time.

Audio finish in a sound dubbing suite

Audio can be sent to a dubbing suite via its original form, for example from the original source tapes, or it can be delivered in a number of digital forms on a hard disk drive.

For a dubbing operation conforming from the original source tapes an EDL is generated and used to control the recapturing of the audio either onto multi-track or, more commonly, into a digital nonlinear audio dubbing system. Digital nonlinear dubbing suites usually have the capability to work directly with audio supplied on a hard disk. This can be a removable hard disk, but it is important that the audio is in a suitable format for the dubbing suite to work with. Common digital audio file formats are AIFF (Audio Interchange File Format) and OMFI (Open Media File Interchange – developed by Avid Technology).

Wherever possible it is a good idea to communicate with the audio suite that is going to be used. They can then advise on the best route to follow, depending on the type of equipment they have and what is the fastest and most economical way to present audio for their use.

Summary

- Audio should always be handled with care.
- Audio sweetening even at a simple level takes time.
- For some programmes audio can be finished in the nonlinear suite.
- If audio is to be sweetened in an audio dubbing suite then check how best to present both the audio and an EDL.

Dubbing suite input options

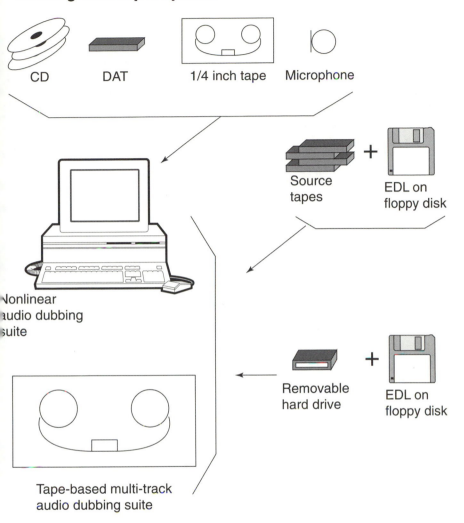

CD DAT 1/4 inch tape Microphone

Source tapes

+ EDL on floppy disk

Nonlinear audio dubbing suite

Removable hard drive

+ EDL on floppy disk

Tape-based multi-track audio dubbing suite

(1) Audio can be supplied as original source material on its own.
(2) Audio supplied as EDL and production video source tapes.
(3) Audio supplied as digital media plus EDL on a floppy disk.

107

Chapter 10

The future

There seems little doubt that digital is here to stay. For broadcasters, this means that the complete chain of acquisition, post-production and transmission will become wholly digital. To some this is the ultimate panacea.

Digital technology is getting cheaper and the quality can be superb, which is fine if everybody uses the same digital encoding systems. However, the nature of the market is such that many different systems will be deployed. The result will inevitably be some confusion.

Digital transmission systems can offer new opportunities. Widescreen transmission is a case in point, coupled with high definition television. This will reduce many existing on-line nonlinear systems to no more than off-line editing systems. While some desktop products are available that offer full uncompressed editing of broadcast images, they are incapable of meeting the data transfer rate required for HDTV. This in itself is not a major restriction as off-line editing has proved to be acceptable as a cost-effective and creative environment for both film and television.

Post-production technology is racing ahead. Many of the criticisms of the existing technology are now being addressed. Both Sony and Panasonic have technologies that support faster than real-time capture of rushes. The existing technology offers up to four times real time. This means a tape with one hour of rushes only takes 15 minutes to be copied to a hard disk drive. It is possible that advances in technology will allow even faster capture rates.

While the above are exciting developments, the greatest development will be the introduction of large server systems which allow many users to access and use the same material simultaneously. Small systems are currently available but it will not be long before all rushes are transferred direct to a server with many users having direct access to all material. Added to this will be the transfer of existing libraries to the server for archive retrieval. Such systems are already beginning to appear, mainly in broadcast newsrooms. It seems likely that as they are developed and proven to be reliable they will become a dominant feature in most broadcasting environments.

While some uncertainty may exist in terms of the precise details of how technology will develop, what is quite clear is that the need for editing will increase – as more and more delivery systems develop, the need for well-edited content will inevitably increase. As the power of desktop nonlinear systems develops so the skill level of its users will also increase.

Appendix A

Glossary

Aliasing Undesirable 'beating' effects caused by sampling frequencies being too low to reproduce image detail faithfully.

Alpha channel Term used to describe an element of a graphics file that will create a hole cutter allowing specified elements of a graphic to be revealed over a background image.

Alpha wrap A method used to wind videotape around a helical scan drum.

Anti-aliasing The smoothing and removing of aliasing effects by filtering and other techniques. Most DVEs and character generators contain anti-aliasing circuitry.

Archive Long-term storage of information. Pictures and sound stored in digital form can be archived and recovered without loss or distortion. The storage medium must be both reliable and stable. As large quantities of information need to be stored, cost is a major consideration. Lowest cost is magnetic tape.

Artefact Particular visible effects which are direct results of some technical limitation. Artefacts are frequently judged on a subjective level. For example, the visual perception of contouring in a picture cannot be described by a signal-to-noise ratio or linearity measurement.

Aspect ratio The ratio of frame width to frame height. The standard aspect ratio for television is 4:3 which closely matches the 16 mm movie film frame. With high definition TV, 16:9 widescreen is also being used.

Assemble (1) To edit on or add material at a point determined by an edit point decision in videotape editing. (See *Auto-assemble* and *Insert editing.*) (2) The recording technique where all recording heads go into record at the same time. Video, audio, timecode and control track all go into record.

Audio and control track head Usually a stationary head on a VTR. This head performs at least two functions: the upper portion serves as the audio head, recording and playing back an audio signal (sometimes there are two or more audio tracks); the lower portion records a control track of pulsed or sinusoidal phase information, which is used to control tape/head rotation speed and phase during playback (very much like the sprocket holes in film).

110

Audio dub To record or re-record the audio portion of a videotape without disturbing the existing video signal or, in some cases, disturbing other audio tracks. (See *Insert editing*)

Auto-assemble Editing handled by an edit controller. The term applies to both VTR (linear) editing and nonlinear editing.

Auto-conform Another term for auto-assemble. When auto-conforming in a linear suite it is essential that the EDL is correct and all the edits are as finally required.

Azimuth The angle of a recording head in relation to audio or videotape. The normal angle is 90 degrees to the direction of the recording track.

Azimuth recording A system of recording where the gaps of the two heads are at different angles to normal. Adjacent tracks are recorded at plus or minus an angle to the normal so that they can be run very close together without interference. It is used on both the Betamax and VHS domestic formats. It is also used in Betacam recorders.

Bandwidth Defines the amount of information that can be passed in a given time. Large bandwidth is needed to show sharp picture detail and is a factor in the quality of recorded or transmitted images. CCIR 601 and SMPTE RP 125 allow analogue luminance bandwidth of 5.5 MHz and chrominance bandwidth of 2.75 MHz, the highest quality attainable in any standard broadcast format. Digital image systems require large bandwidth, hence the reason why many storage and transmission systems use compression techniques to accommodate the signal.

Bearding Artefact associated with poor quality recordings. Identified by black line 'ragging' on high contrast transitions. Usually due to either over-modulation on a recording or worn record/playback heads.

Betacam The trademark for a half-inch professional component videocassette format, developed by Sony.

Binder A chemical that adheres, and at the same time separates iron oxide particles, to videotape backing or base.

Black The darkest of the electronically generated steps of the grey scale. Also called TV Black or 0 V. This 'black' is only as dark as a screen of a television tube when switched off.

Black crushing The pushing of the black recording level so that low-light picture information in the shadows is lost.

Blacked tape A tape that is 'black' or 'blacked' with blanking level and synchronizing information but no active picture information except for control track and timecode. (See *Striped tape*)

111

Black level The bottom level of a video signal, below which are the sync, blanking and other control signals that do not appear as picture information.

Blank tape Unused audio or videotape. Also called virgin tape.

Blanking The electronic beam shut-off period on a television tube during which the line is changed (line blanking), or the next field is changed (filed blanking).

Blanking signal Part of the video signal, which is recorded to indicate the timing and length of time for line and field changes.

Break-up A momentary disruption of a television picture, caused by extraneous electronic signals, loss of primary signal or loss of head-to-tape contact in a recording system.

Burnt-in timecode Timecode that is superimposed on pictures. Useful for off-line selection of footage, or for accurate location when assessing viewing copies of edited items.

Burst The small portion of a video signal that contains approximately 10 cycles of 4.433 MHz colour sub-carrier (PAL) and is used for synchronizing colour throughout the broadcast chain from recording/playback to transmission and reception.

Cassette A self-contained, reel-to-reel cartridge holding either audio or videotape.

CCD scanner A camera/telecine device for the transfer of light to video signal. Charge couple devices (CCD) are now almost exclusively found in TV cameras.

CCIR (Comité Consultatif International de Radio-Communications) This has been absorbed into the ITU under ITU-RCCIR 601 (ITU-R 601). The international standard for digitizing component colour television video in both 525 and 625 line systems, derived from the SMPTE RP125 and the EBU Tech. 3246-E. CCIR 601 deals with both colour difference (Y, R–Y, B–Y) and RGB video, and defines sampling systems, RGB/Y, (R–Y), (B–Y) matrix values and filter characteristics. CCIR 601 is normally taken to refer to colour difference component video (rather than RGB), for which it defines 4:2:2 sampling at 13.5 MHz with 720 luminance samples per active line with 8 or 10 bit digitizing.

Chroma Colour hue and saturation.

Chroma key A method of electronically matting (inserting) an image from one video source into the picture produced by another. The effect is achieved by replacing the colour (often blue but could be any colour) in one scene with another video input. Also called colour separation overlay.

Chroma noise Unwanted random variations of chroma, a

112

common problem with multi-generation videotape recordings.

Chroma output The level of colour output signal recorded. Normally related to the level given by a reference tape.

Chrominance channel The red, green and blue colour channels produced either by a colour camera or a telecine.

Chrominance signal The portion of the total video signal that contains the colour information (R–Y and B–Y), often just referred to as chrominance.

Colour bars An electronically generated video test pattern consisting of vertical bars used to set the chrominance and luminance of cameras and videotape recorders. Colourbars come in a number of standards: 100%, 95% and 75% bars and SMPTE bars.

Colour burst A very accurately phased burst of high frequency (4.433 MHz for PAL) at the beginning of each TV scanning line used to control the reproduced colour of the active picture.

Component (video) A video signal in which the luminance and chrominance remain as separate components, e.g. analogue components in MII and Betacam VTRs, digital components Y, Cr, Cb in CCIR 601. Component signals retain maximum luminance and chrominance bandwidth. Component video is used in Betacam and some digital formats, e.g. D1, D5, Digi Betacam and DVC Pro.

Composite (video) The combination of luminance and chrominance using one of the coding standards – PAL, NTSC and SECAM – to make composite video. The process, which is an analogue form of video compression, restricts the bandwidths (image detail) of components. Chrominance is added to the luminance using a visually acceptable technique but it becomes difficult, if not impossible, to reverse the process (decode) accurately into pure luminance and chrominance.

Compression (video) The process of reducing the amount of bandwidth or data rate for video. The broadcast standards used today – PAL, NTSC and SECAM – are analogue video compression systems. For digital systems, pictures are analysed looking for redundancy and repetition and so discard unnecessary data. The techniques were primarily developed for digital transmission but have been adopted as a means of handling digital video in computers and reducing the storage demands for digital VTRs.

Compression ratio The ratio of the data in the uncompressed digital video signal to the compressed version. Modern compression techniques start with the CCIR 601 component digital signal so the amount of data of the uncompressed video is well defined: 75 GB/hour for 625/50 and 76 GB/hour for the 525/60 standard. The compression ratio should not be used as the only method to

113

assess the quality of a compressed signal. For a given technique, greater compression can be expected to result in worse quality; but different techniques give widely different results for the same compression ratio. The only sure method of judgement is to make a very close inspection of the resulting pictures.

Contouring An unwanted edge or artefact. Digital systems exhibit contouring when insufficient quantizing levels are used or inaccurate processing occurs.

Control track The recorded track which controls by timed pulses the playback speed of the tape and the drum. It is essential for videotape editing.

D1 A format for digital videotape recording working to the CCIR 601 4:2:2 standard using 19 mm wide tape. As a component recording system it is ideal for studio and post-production work. Offers multi-generation capability with little or no picture degradation. Despite this it has not had a large take-up due to high cost.

D2 The standard for digital composite (coded) PAL or NTSC signals. Often used as a direct replacement for 1" VTRs. Although offering good slo-mo modes and multi-generation capabilities, being a coded system means coded characteristics are present, i.e. colour framing sequences.

D3 A VTR standard using ½" tape cassettes for recording digitized composite (coded) PAL or NTSC signals sampled at 8 bits. Characteristics are generally as for D2 except that the small cassette size has allowed a full family of VTR equipment to be developed, including a camcorder.

D5 A VTR format using the same cassette as D3 but recording component signals sampled to CCIR 601 recommendations at 10 bit resolution. With internal decoding D5 VTRs can play back D3 tapes and provide component outputs. Being an uncompressed digital component recorder, D5 enjoys all the benefits of D1, and in addition has provision for HDTV recording using 5:1 compression.

DCT (Discrete Cosine Transform) compression A widely used method of data compression of digital video. Picture information is resolved in blocks (usually 8×8 pixels) into frequencies, amplitudes and colours. JPEG depends on DCT.

Digital disk recorder Disk systems that record digital video. They are typically based on parallel transfer disk drives and offer short duration, around a minute or so, of recording time. They are often used as video caches to provide extra digital video sources for less than the cost of a digital VTR.

Digitizing time Time taken to record footage into a disk-based

114

editing system. Digitizing time is frequently regarded as dead time. With good resource management systems this need not necessarily be so. New technologies are now able to reduce this time (e.g. Panasonic DVCPro and Sony SX).

Dissolve Visual effect performed on a vision mixer. In the videotape post-production environment it requires a three-machine edit suite.

Distortion An unwanted change in an electronic signal, resulting in unfaithful reproduction of audio and/or video signals.

Dropout A loss of picture information and syncs either upon recording or playback. Usually caused by dirt or clogged heads. Identified by white lines across or partly across the television picture or can be exhibited by parts of the reproduced image being filled with noise (black and white dots). Some video players will compensate by repeating the previous line.

Dropout compensator An electronic device that replaces the 'lost' picture information from the previous scanning line. Most professional VTRs are equipped with a dropout compensator.

DT (Dynamic Tracking) or DMC (Dynamic Motion Control) Term used to describe the use of the 'piez' quartz videotape head to produce slow-motion and still frame effects of videotape recorders.

Dub To duplicate or copy audio or videotape masters.

DVE (Digital Video Effects) unit A picture manipulation device allowing both positional and size control of the picture. Some units offer both 2 and 3 dimensional control of the image.

Editing The selection and assembly of a series of scenes to produce a coherent sequence on film or tape.

EDL (Edit Decision List) A list of the decisions, defining a series of edits. Often recorded to a floppy disk. EDLs can be produced during an off-line session and passed to the on-line suite to control the conforming of the final edit.

Electronic Field Production (EFP) The use of portable high quality video recording equipment for on-location productions other than newsgathering.

Electronic News Gathering (ENG) The use of portable video cameras and recorders of high quality to record 'on-the-scene' news reports for television broadcasts. Typically these are now all done with camcorders.

FDDI (Fibre Data Distribution Interface) A high speed fibre optic data interface operating up to 100 Mbits/s.

Field One half of a complete scanning cycle for a picture frame. Two fields are interlaced to form the one frame.

Field sequence A television frame or picture consists of two fields. Each successive frame of component 525 and 625 line television repeats a pattern and so can be edited to frame boundaries – like film editing. Composite video, coded as PAL, NTSC or SECAM, carries colour information on a sub-carrier whose cyclic pattern repeats over a longer period – 4 frames in PAL and 2 frames in NTSC and SECAM – known respectively as the 8 and 4 field sequence. An edit should not break this sequence, by its very nature a less precise operation than with component video. The restrictions apply whether the source is analogue or digital. CCIR 601 component digital signals can edit on any frame boundary while composite digital systems (e.g. D2 or D3 VTRs) are restricted to 4 or 8 field boundaries, otherwise picture hopping or quality changes (through additional processing) will occur.

Frame A complete television picture comprising two fields or a single picture from film.

Frame frequency The number of television pictures per second (30 in NTSC; 25 in PAL and SECAM). Also called frame rate or picture rate. For film this is 24 frames per second.

Freeze frame Motion that is stopped by tracking one field (in some cases a single frame) of video information continuously. Some systems can generate two field freeze frames. Most digital DVEs and nonlinear systems can offer both single-field or both-field freeze frames.

Generation A stage in the duplication of a videotape.

Generation loss The degradation caused by successive recordings or copying of the same material. Every recording or re-recording makes another generation of material (video and/or audio). Recordings straight from the camera are first generation; one re-recording makes the second, as in the first edit of camera rushes. This is a major consideration when working in analogue suites, but less of a consideration in digital suites. The best multi-generation results are possible with disk-based systems recording the uncompressed CCIR 601 signal. With compressed systems there is every chance that digital artifices will accumulate if compressed video crosses too many analogue-to-digital or even inter-coding boundaries.

Glitch A form of low-frequency interference. On a television screen, a glitch appears as a narrow horizontal bar that moves vertically through the picture.

GPI (General Purpose Interface) Usually a switch closure, allowing remote control of external devices on an exact frame. The GPI can be triggered by timecode, giving great accuracy.

GUI (Graphical User Interface) A means of operating a system through the use of interactive graphics displayed on a screen. Examples in the computer world are Apple Mac and Microsoft Windows.

Hard disks (fixed disks) Hard disk drives comprise an assembly of up to 10 rigid platters coated with magnetic oxide, each capable of storing data on both sides. Each recording surface has a write/read head, any one of which may be activated at a given instant. Hard disks give rapid access to vast amounts of data. Hard disk technology is moving very fast with ever-higher capacities becoming available in smaller packages at lower cost per megabyte. Currently for nonlinear editing, hard disk drives are supplied in 4 GB or 9 GB units or even up to 23 GB. Data transfer rates range from 1 to 10 MB/s (SCSI 2) up to 20 MB/s (SCSI Wide).

HDTV (High Definition Television) A television format with a new widescreen aspect ratio of 16:9 (the current is 4:3) and capable of reproducing much more detail (5 to 6 times more) than existing broadcast systems. HDTV should not be confused with widescreen variants of PAL (PALplus), NTCS or SECAM where the screen shape is changed but the quality improvement is small compared with HDTV. Currently there is no agreement for a world HDTV standard. The only consensus so far is that transmission for home viewing and contribution will be digital and compressed, using MPEG 2.

Head A small electromagnetic transducer that reads, writes or erases magnetic signals on an audio or videotape. Video heads are usually in motion, while audio heads are usually stationary.

Headroom (1) Space that should be left between the top of a person's head and the top of frame. (2) In audio, the available gain that could be applied without introducing distortion.

Helical scan A videotape recording system that uses one or two recording heads on a drum to write video information horizontally/transversely in long parallel slants across a tape wrapped in a helix around the drum.

Insert Videotape editing in which only the picture or audio information is replaced but the control track and timecode tracks remain untouched. To insert edit on a blank tape one must first record a control track with timecode, called pre-striping or blacking a tape.

Insert editing The best editing technique to ensure flexibility in selecting tracks to edit on. As a tape editing process, vision, audio and even timecode tracks can be selected in any combination. Requires a pre-blacked tape which has control track, colour black and usually timecode.

ISDN (Integrated Services Digital Network) Allows data to be transmitted at high speed over the public telephone network. ISDN operates from a basic rate of 64 kbits/s up to 2 MB/s. In the television and film industries audio facilities are already using it and some companies have developed systems to allow the exchange of images between machines on a global basis using ISDN. A TV frame takes 2–3 minutes to transmit at the basic rate.

ITU The United Nations regulatory body covering all forms of communication. The ITU sets mandatory standards and regulates the radio frequency spectrum.

Jam sync Method of retaining the synchronicity of timecode when dubbing (copying of tapes) by using a generator to regenerate an identical timecode for the recording. Also should be used with cameras to provide continuous and sequential timecode even if the camera is stopped. Greatly assists in post-production.

Jitter Timebase fluctuations in playback signals due to incorrect reading (or recording) of the control track. The picture quivers horizontally. Can also occur with playback from a hard drive.

JPEG (Joint Photographic Experts Group, ISO/ITU-T) A standard for data compression of still pictures. In particular its work has been involved with pictures coded to the CCIR 601 standard. JPEG uses DCT and offers compression of between 5 and 100 times. Three levels of processing are defined: baseline, extended and 'lossless' encoding. In general, compression can be expected to impose some form of loss or degradation to the picture, its degree depending on the algorithm used as well as the compression ratio and the contents of the picture itself.

Level (1) In video, the signal strength (amplitude) measured in volts. (2) In audio, sound volume measured in decibels.

Line A single trace of the electron beam from left to right across the screen.

Line frequency The number of lines scanned in one second. For PAL, 625 lines at 25 times per second = 15.625 kHz.

118

Logging Making a list of shots. This usually applies to recorded tape or film and can be vital for speeding up the selection of material for editing. This is especially true when going to a disk-based system where digitizing time can be a minimum. The list or log can be on paper or a computer floppy disk. When on disk great savings can be made during the digitizing process. Examples are media log and Phoenix log.

LTC (Longitudinal Timecode) Timecode recorded on a linear track on tape and read by a static head. This timecode can be read when the tape is moving forwards or backwards but cannot be read when the tape is stationary.

Luminance A component, the black and white or brightness element, of an image. It is written Y, so the Y in YUV, YIQ, (Y, R–Y, B–Y) and Y, Cr, Cb is the luminance information of the signal. In a colour TV system the luminance is usually derived from the RGB signals, originating from the camera, by a matrix or summation of approximately: $Y = 0.3R + 0.6G + 0.1B$.

Luminance channel A signal that is derived from the three chrominance channels to produce the basic black and white signal.

Match frame Term used to indicate correct matching of source material back onto itself, having already been edited. For example, a shot already used in a programme needs to be re-edited back into the programme at exactly the same place so that a name super can be added.

Monitor A high quality television set without a tuner, used to display directly composite video or R, G and B signals.

MPEG 1 and 2 (Moving Picture Experts Group, ISO/ITU-T) MPEG is involved in defining a standard for the data compression of moving pictures. Its work follows on from that of JPEG to add interfield compression, the extra compression potentially available through similarities between successive frames of moving pictures. MPEG 1 was originally designed to work at 1.2 MB/s, the data rate of CD-ROM, so that video could be played from CDs. However, the quality is not sufficient for TV broadcast. MPEG 2 has been designed to cover a wide range of requirements from VHS quality all the way up to HDTV through a series of algorithm 'profiles' and image resolution 'levels' with data rates generally between 2 and 10 Mbits/s.

Noise An unwanted electrical disturbance or random signal that creates extraneous sound or picture signal interference. In video,

119

noise shows up on the TV screen as 'snow'. Analogous to grain in film.

Nonlinear editing Means of off-line editing using picture and sound information digitized to a hard drive computer system, e.g. Avid, Edit, Media 100 and Lightworks. More and more these systems are being used to finish the programme for transmission.

NTSC (National Television Standards Committee) Defined the 525 line 60 fields per second standard for television used in the USA and Japan.

Off-line (editing) A decision-making process using low-cost equipment to produce an EDL or a rough cut which can then be conformed or referred to in a high quality on-line suite. This cuts down the cost of a production by removing the decision-making from the expensive post-production environment. While in the past most off-line suites would enable the selection of shots and the defining of transitions such as cuts and dissolves, very few would allow the setting of DVEs, colour correction or keyers. The modern systems now offer these facilities, e.g. Avid, Edit, Lightworks, Quantel.

Omega wrap A configuration of videotape that has been wound around a helical scan drum. (See also *Alpha wrap.*)

OMFI (Open Media Framework Interchange) A specification for media interchange between a range of equipment. In principle OMFI is an open, public standard file format for digital media interchange between applications which supports video, audio, graphics, animation and CG. It will also contain all descriptive data representing all editing decisions, how media is organized and how a programme is to be played. It also offers multi-platform compatibility. A powerful concept that is gaining momentum, with several manufacturers now actively involved, e.g. Avid, AMS Neve, Digidesign, Studer, Synclavir.

On-line (editing) An edit suite where the final edit is performed in full programme quality. Being higher quality than off-line, time costs more. Preparation in the off-line will save time and money in the on-line.

PAL (Phase Alternating Line) The system devised in West Germany and Britain as one standard for 625 line 50 fields per second colour television.

Parallel transfer drives These are a variant of Winchester disks with enhanced electronics allowing each of the read/write heads to operate simultaneously. This allows data to be transferred to or from the disk at very high speeds (approximately 10 to 20 MB/s). With careful design and special interfacing, these drives can be used for random access real-time video storage.

Persistence The length of time a phosphor dot glows on a television screen or flying spot telecine: longer for the former, extremely short for the latter.

Pixel The name given to one sample of picture information. A shortened version of 'picture cell' or 'picture element'. Pixel can refer to an individual sample of R, G, B, luminance or chrominance, or sometimes to a collection of such samples if they are cosited and together produce one picture element.

Playback To operate an audio or videotape recorder in a 'read' mode to give sound and/or picture images.

Post-dubbing The process of adding a sound track to a recorded – and usually edited – videotape recording.

Pre-roll The process of running two or more tapes in synchronization in preparation for an electronic edit. The pre-roll time is usually 5 seconds in Betacam edit suites. Some nonlinear edit systems also offer this capability, but it is not really an appropriate process within the nonlinear environment and performing a basic edit. However, there are situations where pre-roll does have its place in the nonlinear environment.

PTC (Piece to Camera) or Standupper Used to describe a sync piece of dialogue spoken direct to camera. A favourite with journalists.

Quantizing (quantization) The process of sampling an analogue waveform to provide packets of digital information representing the original signal.

RAID (Redundant Array of Industry standard (or Inexpensive) Drives) A grouping of standard disk drives together with a controller to provide performance beyond that available from individual drives. RAIDs can offer very high capacities, fast data transfer rates and much increased security of data. The latter is achieved through disk redundancy so that disk errors or failures can be corrected or masked.

Random access (editing) The ability to read any frame at any time, with instant access and no restrictions on dubbing time during the actual editing process. Random access is a completely new way of working, freeing one from the restrictions of linear working.

Raster The pattern formed by the scanning spot on the face

121

of a cathode ray tube. It creates the illumination area of the tube.

Resolution A measure of the finest detail that can be seen, or resolved, in a reproduced image. Whilst it is influenced by the number of pixels in an image (e.g. HDTV approx. 2000 × 1000, broadcast TV 720 × 576 or 720 × 487), the pixel numbers do not define ultimate resolution but merely the resolution of that part of the equipment. The quality of lenses, cameras, display tubes, film scanners, etc. used to produce the image on the screen must all be taken into account.

Resolution-independent Term used to describe the notion of equipment that can operate at any or many resolutions. Dedicated TV equipment is designed to operate at a single resolution although some modern equipment can switch between the specific formats and aspect ratio of 525/60 and 626/50. Computers by their nature can handle files of any size so, when applied to imaging, they are termed resolution-independent.

Rotary erase head An erase head incorporated into the rotating drum of a recorder. Essential for perfect electronic editing. Also called a flying erase head.

Sampling Process applied to convert an analogue signal into a series of digital values.

Sampling standard A standard for sampling analogue wave-forms to convert them into digital data. The official sampling standard for television is CCIR 601 (now known as ITU-R 601).

Scan One horizontal electron beam sweep across a television camera target, picture tube or flying spot scanner. A scan is accomplished in 64 microseconds (PAL).

Scanning The continuous movement of the electron beam as it scans across a cathode ray tube from left to right and from top to bottom.

SCSI (Small Computer Systems Interface) A high data-rate general-purpose parallel interface. A maximum of 8 devices can be connected to one bus, for example a controller and up to 7 disks or devices of different sorts – Winchester disks, optical disks, tape drives, etc. – and may be shared between several computers. SCSI specifies a cabling standard (50 way), a protocol for sending and receiving commands and their format. It is intended as a device-independent interface so the host computer needs no details about the peripherals it controls. But with two versions (single-ended and differential/balanced), many connector types and numerous variations in the level of implementation of the

122

interface, SCSI devices cannot be 'plug and play' on a computer with which they have not been tested. Also with total bus cabling for the popular single-ended configuration limited to 6 metres all devices must be close together. Standard SCSI has a maximum data transfer rate of nearly 5 MB/s. SCSI 2 offers faster transfer rates (up to 10 MB/s) and an extended set of commands. SCSI Wide has a 16 bit bus allowing data transfers of up to 20 MB/s.

SECAM (Séquential Couleur à Mémoire) The French colour television transmisson system using 625 lines and 50 fields per second. Also adopted in eastern Europe.

Serial control Generally used to describe remote control of a device via a data line. The control is transmitted down the line in serial form, i.e. one control signal after another. Frequently used in the RS 422 form for control between VTRs, vision mixers and DVEs.

Serial digital interface (SDI) The standard based on a 270 Mbits/s transfer rate. This is a 10 bit, scrambled, polarity independent interface, with common scrambling for both component CCIR 601 and composite digital video and four channels of (embedded) digital audio. Most new broadcast digital equipment includes SDI, which greatly simplifies the installation of equipment and signal distribution.

Servo Used to control the tape and head speeds from the control track pulses.

Signal-to-noise The ratio of the strength of a video signal (S) to the accompanying electronic interference (noise, N). The higher the S/N ratio (more signal, less noise) the better the quality of the resulting sound or video. S/N ratios are expressed in dB.

Still picture Produced when the tape is stopped and the video heads are made to play back the same tracks on the tape continuously. On most player/recorders there is a loss of resolution in the reproduced picture. Still frame should not be left on for too long or tape damage/head wear will be accelerated. Most recorders have a pre-set shut-down time at which point tape tension is reduced round the heads to prevent these problems. On digital recorders it is strongly recommended that the tape be removed from the transport when not being used. This is due to the very small size of the head gap of digital recorders, and there is a possibility on some digital machines that the video head drum will not spin down until tapes are removed.

Striped tape A term used to describe videotape pre-recorded with colour black and burst. The tape will have a continuous control track and uninterrupted timecode recorded along its entire length. This is the tape that would be used in the recorder for insert editing.

Sync Short for synchronization. The electronic pulses (vertical and horizontal) that synchronize the scanning in a camera, VTR or flying spot telecine with the scanning in a monitor. The sync pulses can be derived internally, i.e. from the video signal, or externally from a sync generator.

Sync pulse The electronic pulse produced by a sync generator and entered into the video signal during the blanking interval to ensure exact synchronization.

Sync signal A series of sync pulses is the composite video signal.

Talking head A single shot of someone talking. Usually used to describe interviews or PTCs (Piece to Camera).

Tape An audio or video recording medium consisting of a poly-ester or mylar base, a binder, and a suspension in the binder of magnetizable particles such as ferric oxide or chromium dioxide. The tape is approximately 25 microns thick. Standard widths are ¼″, 8 mm, ½″, ¾″ and 1″. Modern digital formats go down to 6 mm in width.

Tape speed The rate at which tape passes over the fixed head (audio) of a recorder. The rate differs from format to format.

Termination A load inserted to a transmission line used to keep the signal from bouncing back (reflections) along the line. In video, the terminator is a 75 ohm resister and must be inserted or switched in at the end of a video chain. Also used to end the chain of SCSI hard drives on nonlinear edit systems.

Timecode A digital signal recorded onto tape providing a refer-ence for all frames recorded on that tape. The reference provided is in units of hours:minutes:seconds:frames (note that in the PAL TV system there are 25 frames per second). After the invention of the videotape recorder, timecode was the next most significant development. It provides two vital elements to post-production: accuracy and repeatability.

Tracking (1) The angle and speed at which a video head passes across the tape. (2) The accuracy with which a playback head follows the correct recording path across the tape.

U-matic Trade name for the ¾″ videocassette format developed by Sony Corporation. Available in three formats: High Band SP and High Band used for broadcast and Low Band used in educational and industrial applications. Now largely a redundant format with

124

the arrival of low budget Beta SP and semi-pro digital formats.

Vapourware Software or hardware that is promised or talked about but is not yet completed – and may never be realized.

VCR Videocassette recorder or video cartridge recorder.

Vectorscope An electronic display device, similar to an oscilloscope, used to visually measure the amplitude and phase of the R, G and B television colour signals.

Video The picture and sync pulse portions of a television signal. Often used to refer to the recording of television pictures.

Video head The recording or playback head which transfers the video signal to and from the tape.

Video signal Television picture frequencies ranging from 0 up to 5.5 MHz. It is an amplified signal containing picture information, sync and blanking pulses.

VITC (Vertical Interval Timecode) Timecode data in digital form, integrated as part of the vision information on tape. This can be read by the video heads at any time that pictures are displayed, even during jogging and freeze but not during spooling. This complements LTC, ensuring timecode can be read at all times there is head (audio/video) to tape contact.

VTR (Videotape Recorder) The electromechanical device used to record television images, audio signals and control information on magnetically coated tape. Also used to play back for viewing or editing.

Waveform monitor An oscilloscope used to analyse and adjust television signal characteristics visually. Usually displays the R, G and B signals separately on the same screen. Can also display full coded PAL signal sometimes useful in the editing suite for an overall picture of signals as they will be replayed.

Winchester A particular form of hard disk which has several disk platters and their associated heads sealed in a dust-free enclosure. It offers high reliability and a high data-packing density.

Wipe Visual effect performed on a vision mixer. Most mixers offer over 30 different wipe patterns, most with border or softness as additional controls.

WORM (1) Write Once/Read Many – a type of storage device on which data once written cannot be erased or rewritten. Being optical, WORMs offer very high recording densities and are removable making them in some applications useful for archiving. WORMs have not made a significant impact in the post-production world, mainly due to the slow transfer rates currently available for the optical WORMS. (2) Type of virus, found on Macintosh computers.

Writing speed The relative speed between the heads and the tape during recording and playback. In audio where the heads are fixed the speed of the tape is the writing speed. In video the speed of the heads rotating on the periphery of the drum is virtually the writing speed. The relationship of writing speed and head gap determines the maximum frequency recordable and played back.

Y, (R–Y), (B–Y) Analogue luminance, Y, and colour difference signals (R–Y) and (B–Y) of component video. Y is pure luminance information and the two colour difference signals are the colour information. The signals are derived from the original RGB source. The Y, (R–Y), (B–Y) signals are fundamental to much of television. For example, in CCIR 601 (or more correctly ITU-R 601) it is these signals that are digitized to make 4:2:2 component digital video and in PAL and NTSC TV systems they are used to generate the final composite coded signal. When digitized, the convention is to designate the signals as Y, Cr, Cb.

Z axis The third dimension of the three-dimensional world. The Z axis is at right angles to the X and Y axes. A control offered on 3-D picture manipulation devices.

Zits Slang for short-term errors in digital recordings.

Appendix B

Edit decision lists

As stated earlier, EDLs are one of the options of output from a non-linear system. This is still a popular way of working. That is, a low-cost nonlinear system performs the off-line edit and an EDL is generated and sent with the source tapes to the on-line linear tape edit suite for finishing or auto-conforming. All professional nonlinear systems offer the ability to generate EDLs. Some use stand-alone software packages and others have integrated applications. Whichever is available, certain guidelines need to be followed. If not, there is the risk that the on-line edit will become an expensive and embarrassing exercise.

If working on a programme which is going to be edited as an off-line project and subsequently going to be auto-conformed in a tape-to-tape suite, then preparation for the on-line starts at the point that you start the off-line. The reason is quite simple – you are going into a tape-to-tape suite, so all your media, that is graphics, voice-overs, music, must be on timecoded tapes. Any media arriving on floppies, audiocassette or ¼" tape should be compiled onto a timecoded source tape before loading into the nonlinear system for the off-line edit. If this is not done then the EDL created will be unusable by the on-line edit suite.

Another point to remember is that most on-line edit controllers do not like tape names with alphanumerics. While some can handle alphanumerics, all can cope with simple numerics. So, wherever possible, organize source tapes with a simple numbering system. In fact some older controllers will only support a two-digit numbering system, i.e. 01, 02, 03, ..., 99. To play safe and keep things simple, label all tapes with a chinagraph pencil and where necessary create a basic look-up table of the original tape name and the numbering system that has been used. As with all things, preparation is everything!

Assuming the above preparation has been done we can now look at what an EDL is and examine some of the limitations. An EDL is little more than a list of text statements indicating which shot from which tape was used and where it is on the programme tape. When it comes to effects, the dissolve and, maybe, some wipes might be supported in the on-line suite. However, digital effects and multiple layers of video will not be.

On-line edit suites frequently have equipment from a number of manufacturers, from the edit controller and vision mixer to the digital video effects device (DVE). As a consequence the level of communication between all this equipment will be at a very primitive level. This means that EDLs of necessity have to be very basic.

Before making an EDL there are a number of questions that need to be asked. For example:

- What edit controller is being used in the on-line suite?
- What vision mixer does the on-line suite have?
- What sort mode does the on-line editor require?

It is important to know what edit controller is going to be used, as edit controllers from different manufacturers are basically incompatible. So the list must be made in the right format for the edit controller in question, be it Sony, Ampex, Paltex, CMX, GVG (and this list is by no means exhaustive!). In addition it might be worth knowing what level of software the edit controller has installed. One area where many first-time off-line editors get caught is the floppy disk size. Quite a few edit controllers still only accept EDLs on a double density disk (800 kB). Trying to get hold of a double density disk can sometimes be difficult – most floppy disks nowadays are high density disks (1.4 MB), which cannot be read by some edit controllers. If faced with this problem, it is possible to take a high density disk and mask off the hole which does not have the write-protect tab. The Mac or Wintel machine will see this disk as a double density disk. You will need to format the disk as a 800 kB disk and then save your EDL to the disk.

Knowing what vision mixer is used might be helpful as some do conform to SMPTE wipe codes. If not, be prepared to add comments to the EDL for the on-line editor.

Sometimes on-line editors will request a particular sort mode for the EDL, based on the length of the programme and the source tapes. The different sort modes are as follows.

Sort mode A

This is the simplest sort mode to understand, but not necessarily the fastest to perform in the on-line edit. The A sort mode is linear, so that when the auto-conform begins it records the first shot of the show, then the second, and so on until the programme is complete. Any effects, for example dissolves, are performed as they are encountered from the EDL.

Sort mode B
This sort mode might be preferred when the programme length is longer than the source tapes. It is primarily of value for long form shows. During the auto-conform a source tape is loaded and it fast forwards and rewinds, finding the required shots and dropping them in the appropriate place on the record master tape. While potentially faster than A mode it can be confusing to watch, as the record master will initially have a lot of black holes, which can be disconcerting for both client and the editor. However, if the EDL is 'solid' then there are speed advantages.

Sort mode C
In this mode the record tape shuttles up and down, grabbing the shots it requires as the source tape steps through from beginning to end. This process is typically used when the source tape is longer than the record master, for example when compiling a movie trailer, or a promotions menu where three drama series are being previewed in a one-minute trailer.

Sort modes D and E
These are variations on the B and C sort modes. Here the effects are all performed as the last edits of the auto-conform. It is frequently not a popular choice unless the on-line edit suite is very well lined up, because the D and E modes do not track which videotape player made an original edit. This means that at the end of the list when the effects are created, the edit controller may well ask for a source tape to be loaded into a different playback machine from the original edit. If machines are not all perfectly matched and the tape line-up performed to the same exacting level, the match frame edit required for the effect will not be invisible.

Modes B to E are sometimes referred to as **checkerboard editing**, due to the record master having lots of black holes at the beginning of the process. Nevertheless, for a solid EDL, time can be saved.

Further considerations
As nonlinear systems support multiple vision and audio tracks, it may be necessary to create several EDLs because the on-line edit

controller will not support multiple tracks in the EDL. In the case of multiple vision tracks, an EDL for each additional vision track will need to be created. In the on-line suite these additional EDLs will be auto-conformed first to create a series of sub-masters, which can then be played in during the on-line edit as required. For audio, up to four audio tracks can usually be supported, although older controllers may only support two audio tracks.

There is a need to be careful when creating motion effects. Nonlinear systems typically support a greater range than can be supported by a single pass on a videotape deck. There will also be the need to create a duplicate reel list. This list is required for all those dissolves, etc. that occur between two shots which exist on the same source tape. For a tape-to-tape suite to perform a simple dissolve in this situation a copy of one of the shots must be on a separate tape. If a digital suite is to be used then the duplicate reel list might not be required as most digital tape decks support what is known as pre-read. This facility allows a digital recorder to play back before the record head (or pre-read), so that the digital recorder can replay the end of the last shot and record the same information as the dissolve to the new source takes place. However, once this is done it is a major task to change the transition.

The most important thing to remember is that changes should not be made in the on-line – on-line edit suite time is not cheap. To maximize the benefit of the automated process of auto-conforming on tape the EDL must be well prepared, bearing in mind the limitations of on-line tape-to-tape linear editing.

Appendix C

Recording formats and what they offer

All the formats and systems covered in this appendix have tried to address one or more of the following requirements of the programme maker and broadcaster:

* compact size;
* relatively low cost;
* faster transfer rates;
* future proof, e.g. widescreen capable.

Digi-Betacam

Digi-Betacam is presently Sony's flagship recording technology. The system uses a discrete cosine transform (DCT) process with bit rate reduction (BRR). This sounds very technical but in essence this technology provides very high quality images while using a small degree of compression (2:1). On the high end systems dual aspect ratios are supported: 4:3 and 16:9. Widescreen is an interesting aspect with digital technology and has implications for both production and post-production.

The format offers four independently accessible high quality audio tracks, as well as timecode tracks.

One other feature of Digi-Betacam is its backward compatibility to Beta SP, i.e. Beta SP tapes can be played back on a Digi-Betacam machine (if you have the right model!).

As a product it has proved to offer high quality and reliability, but at a cost. It is not cheap and maintenance can be expensive.

Digi-Betacam has been around for some time and as such is not really one of the 'new' formats that are flooding the market.

DVCPro (25)

DVCPro (25) is Panasonic's offering of a cost-effective solution to electronic field production (EFP) and electronic news gathering (ENG). Panasonic has offered the recording as an open technology, which third party manufacturers can also use. For example, Avid, Truevision and Montage have developed capture cards that will accept the DVCPro format directly.

131

The format uses a small ¼" tape, with tape transports and processing offering backward compatibility to the domestic DV format. The recording system is proprietary but is based on an intraframe compression process. This accommodates frame-accurate editing. Compression is applied at the level of 5:1 and the data rate is 25 Mbits/s.

While the DVCPro (25) only supports two audio tracks on tape it does offer 4 × real-time transfer rates for editing. In effect 12 minutes of rushes can be transferred to hard disk in 3 minutes – an attractive feature, particularly in fast turnaround environments such as news, sport and current affairs.

DVCPro (50)

This is the big brother to the DVCPro (25). As the 50 in its name implies it offers higher data rates and less compression (3:1). As such the DVCPro (50) is aimed at high-end productions. The family includes products offering switchable widescreen aspect ratios and high definition TV formats. The DVCPro (50) is also backward compatible to the DVCPro (25). Four audio tracks are supported, as well as 2 × real-time transfer of data to hard drive.

DVCAM

This is Sony's offering at the semi-pro level. The format uses a 5:1 compression ratio, with faster than real-time digitizing, when used with Sony's proprietary digitizing cards. The compression process is intraframe, allowing frame-accurate editing. Audio is switchable between 2 and 4 audio tracks, the 2 audio track option using 16 bit quantization and 48 kHz sampling. If in 4 audio track mode the quantizing is based on 12 bits and a sampling frequency of 38 kHz. Studio playback machines will also play back consumer DV format tapes.

Betacam SX

Here Sony have opted for an interframe compression system, based on MPEG 2. Compression is applied at a level of 10:1. Four digital audio tracks are available, all high quality, using 16 bit quantization and 48 kHz sampling.

The format also offers a useful shot logging system that will allow 'OK' or 'NG' (no good) takes to be logged. These references aid fast identification of all the good takes when editing. Widescreen (16:9) and normal 4:3 aspect ratios are selectable. The only real question mark over the format is the use of MPEG 2 encoding.

Digital S

Digital S is JVC's successor to VHS. This is a high quality format. While using an MPEG 2 compression process JVC have wisely incorporated an intraframe component for frame-accurate editing. The compression is applied at approximately 3:1. Two or 4 audio tracks are selectable and the players are backward compatible with S-VHS tapes.

Broadcast Recordable Video CD

This offers nonlinear access to rushes – what every editor wants. At the moment, though, only prototype products have been demonstrated. NEC have shown a system using MPEG encoding. The main problem is that of gyroscopic movement of the camera during recording. When a solution is found, such a system would be very popular for fast turnaround productions such as news and sport, offering shoot and record to a CD and random access to the rushes for editing.

Avid/Ikegami

The Camcutter also offers instant access to rushes. Here the recording medium is a hard disk. The system uses JPEG compression for the video with four digital audio tracks. When the 'field pac' or dockable hard disk is plugged into the Avid Newscutter, the editor then has instant access to the rushes. While the system has been used successfully, the cost of the field pacs has probably restricted its use on a wider scale.

DV

This consumer format, targeted at replacing VHS and HI 8, is a digital format offering very good quality pictures and better multi-generation capabilities than its analogue equivalents. Compression is 5:1 and two audio tracks are available. As noted above, both Panasonic and Sony are offering compatibility (for playback) on their professional systems.

Further reading

Bayes, Steve, *The Avid Handbook*, Focal Press, Oxford, 1998.
Browne, Steven E., *Nonlinear Editing Basics*, Focal Press, Oxford, 1998.
Browne, Steven E., *Video Editing* (Third edition), Focal Press, Oxford, 1998.
Case, Dominic, *Film Technology in Post Production*, Focal Press, Oxford, 1997.
Dancyger, Ken, *The Technique of Film and Video Editing*, Focal Press, Oxford, 1997.
Murch, Walter, *In the Blink of an Eye*, Silman-James Press, 1995.
Ohanian, Thomas A., *Digital Nonlinear Editing* (Second edition), Focal Press, Oxford, 1998.
Pank, Bob, *The Digital Fact Book* (Sixth edition), Quantel, 1996.
Rumsey, Francis and McCormick, Tim, *Sound and Recording – An Introduction* (Second edition), Focal Press, Oxford, 1996.
Thompson, Roy, *The Grammar of the Edit*, Focal Press, Oxford, 1997.

Visit our web site for:

- the latest information on new and forthcoming Focal Press titles
- special offers
- our e-mail news service

Join our Focal Press Bookbuyers Club____

As a member, you will enjoy the following benefits:

- special discounts on new and best-selling titles
- advance information on forthcoming Focal Press books
- a quarterly newsletter highlighting special offers
- a 30-day guarantee on purchased titles

Membership is free. To join, supply your name, company, address, telephone/fax numbers and e-mail address to:
Elaine Hill
E-mail: elaine.hill@repp.co.uk
Fax: +44(0) 1865 314423
Address: Focal Press, Linacre House, Jordan Hill, Oxford OX2 8DP

Catalogue____

For information on all Focal Press titles, we will be happy to send you a free copy of the Focal Press Catalogue.

Tel: 01865 314693
E-mail: carol.burgess@repp.co.uk

Potential authors____

If you have an idea for a book, please get in touch:

Europe
Beth Howard, Editorial Assistant
E-mail: beth.howard@repp.co.uk
Tel: +44 (0) 1865 314365
Fax: +44 (0) 1865 314572

USA
Marie Lee, Publisher
E-mail: marie.lee@bhusa.com
Tel: 781 904 2500
Fax: 781 904 2620